FEAR AND FASCINATION

THE 100 BEST ROCK CLIMBS IN ENGLAND AND WALES

Fear and Fascination

THE 100 BEST ROCK CLIMBS
IN ENGLAND AND WALES

GEOFFREY ODDS

The Crowood Press

First published in 1994 by
The Crowood Press Ltd
Ramsbury, Marlborough
Wiltshire SN8 2HR

British Library Cataloguing-in-Publication Data

A catalogue record for this book is available from the British Library.

ISBN 1 85223 607 8

Picture Credits

All photographs by the author except for those supplied by the following: Richie Brooks, pages 112, 122, 145 and colour plate 14 (bottom); Paul Cornforth, page 140; Mark Edwards, page 38 and colour plate 5 (bottom); Rowland Edwards, pages 12, 35, 40, 41, 50 and 51; Paul Harrison, page 49 (both); Dave Hauton, pages 30–1 and colour plate 4; Alan James, page 61; Dave Kendall, pages 32 (bottom), 84 and colour plate 11; Steve Lewis, pages 68, 69 and colour plate 15; Pete Oxley, page 21 and colour plate 2 (top); Simon Pease, page 113 and colour plate 13; Chris Plant, page 62 and colour plate 7 (top); Ben Pritchard, pages 80, 82 and colour plate 9 (bottom); Sue Simpson, page 120 and colour plate 14 (top); Nick White, pages 27, 28, 48 and colour plate 3; Gary Wickham, pages 20, 22, 63 and colour plate 6; Bob Wightman, page 141; Ray Wood, pages 72, 72–3, 78, 81 (both), 85, 90, 96 and colour plates 7 (bottom), 8, 9 (top), 10 (both). Frontispiece shows Chequers Buttress (climber Peter Menke); page 8 shows High Tor. Photographs by the author.

Typeset by Phoenix Typesetting, Ilkley, West Yorkshire.
Printed and bound in Great Britain at The Bath Press.

Contents

Preface   6

Acknowledgements   7

Introduction   9

The Routes:

   The South and West   15

   Wales   53

   The North   98

Information   149

Glossary   157

Index of Climbs   160

Preface

This book has been on the go now for five years; the idea originally formed while I worked away as an accountant in an office in Slough. To my surprise the third publisher I approached gave me a contract and I was in business. I had thought to myself that this would be a good way of doing a lot more climbing with some definite end product in mind. I envisaged myself spending long days climbing while others worked. The reality was somewhat different. I had eighteen months to do the book, but the first twelve were wiped out by the recurrence of a mystery virus I had picked up in Pakistan. No matter, I still had plenty of time. Of course I was not planning on meeting with such awful weather. I would arrange to photograph a climb only for it to rain, and the subjects would then be unavailable for another week; what I had thought would be easy turned into very hard work. I spent my time either on the phone hassling people to do routes so that I could photograph them, or travelling around the country with an assortment of people climbing and taking pictures. When you're hanging halfway up the main cliff of Gogarth and it's windy and you've been there all day and you're cold and tired, the good old office doesn't seem such a bad place. Well actually it does, and I am really very grateful for having had this opportunity to do something different. In my travels and during my travails, I have met a lot of people who have been extremely helpful and put themselves out for very little reward: to these people, many of whom have become friends, I am also very grateful. I hope that you, the reader, will enjoy this book; a lot of work has gone into it and I hope that it hasn't been wasted. If it inspires just one of you to get out and do one of these climbs it will have been worth it. Happy reading, and above all, happy and safe climbing.

Acknowledgements

I would like to thank the following companies and individuals for their invaluable help and support in the production of this book: Wild Country, for supplying me with Rocks, Friends, karabiners, boots, slings and quick draws, all of which I found to be excellent in use; Lyon Equipment, for supplying me with Petzl harnesses and a Shunt, which proved invaluable when abbing for pictures; Mark Pretty, for being an enthusiast, and giving me everyone else's phone numbers; Gary Wickham, for being very patient while helping me to climb better – 'If I was to say undercut would it mean anything to you?'; and Corinne Chapman.

And now the cast of thousands, listed in no particular order: Steve Anson, 'Dodgy' Dave Hauton, 'Slow' Nick Hepburn, Nick Barraclough, Kath Gil, Jane Stannard, Ian Smith, Hilary Got, Mat Saunders, Nigel Fawthrop, Zoe Panchic, Nick Mathews, Alison Mathews, Felicity Butler, Fred Simpson, Sue Simpson, Ben Moon, Jerry Moffat, John Welford, Robin Barker, Andy Popp, Nick Dixon, Paul Pritchard, Nick Harms, Carolyn Tickel, Zoe Brown, Ben Pritchard, Rowland Edwards, Mark Edwards, Gary Gibson, Nick White, Dave Thomas, Richie Brooks, David 'book author' Jones, Pat Jones, Steve Gorton, John Arran, Tony Ryan, Paul Cornforth, Paul Harrison, Pete Bull, Sean Myles, Chris Plant, Fiona Lloyd, Gareth Jones, Jasper Sharpe, Ray Wood, Dave Kendall, Mike Eden, Pete Oxley, Martin Crocker, Dominic Cook, Martin Crook, Alistair Hopkins, Sabina Gutte, Peter Menke, Mat Smith, Bill Whatley, Alan James, John Leach, Adam Wainwright, Simon Nadin, Steve 'the pro' Lewis, Bob Wightman, Dave Towse, Mike Turner, Dave Turner. If you aren't here and you helped then I'm sorry, but thanks anyway.

I would also like to pay a personal tribute to two climbers who recently died before their time: Ed Stone and Rachel Farmer. I knew neither that closely, although I had known Ed for many years, but found them to share two things in common, a joy of life and an unbounded enthusiasm for climbing. Their enthusiasm rubbed off on everyone who met them and it is tragic that they have been taken from us. I will miss them both.

Introduction

There have been many books published about rock climbing in this country. Detailed guide-books to all the crags, selected guidebooks to all the areas, books of prose, books of fiction, books about technique, books about training and others about the people involved and picture books about routes.

This book falls into the last category but is different from those that have preceded it. Previous exaltations of British climbing have concentrated on 'classic' climbs at various grades. This book concentrates only on the very 'best' routes, regardless of their place in climbing history. This book, unlike others that have come before it, sets out to tell you, the reader, which are the 100 best routes to climb in England and Wales, regardless of grade or historic importance.

Some of the routes contained within may also come into the 'classic' category. This means that not only are they established routes and have some historic significance but are also excellent climbs when compared to those that have come before or since. There are many famous climbs that have become established as the best routes that are not in this book. Why? Because they aren't as good as those that are contained in the book. Why then does everyone think they are the best? Well, it's a self-perpetuating cycle: a route is done, it is a breakthrough at the time or is well publicized and accessible, so more people go and do it. Then these people, because they have been told it is good and want it to be, have a good time and tell others the route is good, who then go and climb it, and so the cycle starts again. At this point though I should make it clear that I have not done all the routes in England and Wales. I do not imagine anyone has or that anyone ever will. I have not even done all the routes in the book as my climbing ability does not extend to the loftier grades. This might then prompt the question, how did I arrive at these particular 100 routes? The process involved several stages over a period of two years.

First I asked as many people as I could find to tell me what they thought the best routes they had done were. Then, I ploughed through all the guide-books searching for brilliant-sounding, less well-known routes. I then compiled a list and sent it to as many people as I could, asking for their opinions. After that, I modified my list and started on the process of climbing, photographing and writing about the routes. While doing this I asked as many people as I could, who were active in the various areas and who had local knowledge that I couldn't hope to have, to give me their opinion of what was good in their area. A case in point is my trip to Pembroke, where my preconceived list changed over the space of five days and the fabulous Pigs on the Wing was pointed out to me. Then, having re-evaluated the list, I compared area to area and grade to grade, and routes within the same area and routes within the same grade, before eventually arriving at the 100 routes laid before you.

What is so good about each route will, I hope, become clear in the photographs and text. I have not tried to give a justification for each route's inclusion, but I have tried to express, either through a description or a narration of personal experience, what makes the climb so excellent.

There is something to suit every taste in this list, and this is the beauty of climbing in England

and Wales. The huge variety of rock types, climbing styles and environments is difficult to match anywhere else in the world in such a small area. Bold routes, bolt routes, easy routes, hard routes, short routes and long routes are all here. Routes above the sea, routes in mountains, routes on moors, routes in river valleys, routes on little crags in wooded glades and routes in quarries wait to be climbed. There are routes on sandstone, gritstone, limestone, granite, slate and chalk.

So what is the point to this book, or is it just another ticklist? Well, yes, it is another ticklist but it will be someone quite exceptionally dedicated who ticks all these routes. The book is intended to give a definitive list of the best climbs in England and Wales. It should provoke debate and should lead people to new areas and to routes they may not have considered previously. The book is a celebration of the very best climbing that England and Wales have to offer.

So I hope the remainder of the book will interest you, stimulate you and make you want to get out of the gym and on to the rock. I also hope that if you climb any of the routes in this book you will not be disappointed. I am sure you may have picked some different routes for your personal 'best 100' but I hope that I have not included any that you will think are rubbish. These are the best, so why not do the best before the rest?

ETHICS

Ethics are a personal matter. They have to be, as they cannot be enforced by any organization but only by individuals. Ethics are the set of rules we use to guide our actions.

Climbers as a whole have a strong sense of ethics. These ethics change as society changes, as the sport changes. It is the case, however, that what is considered OK by one person is abhorrent to another, and it is because of this and the fact there are no rules in rock climbing, that climbers spend an awful lot of time discussing ethics.

I would like to discuss here a few of the more commonly debated issues, and by doing so maybe compile a list of ethical values that you might find useful.

Bolts

The biggest argument in climbing today, as we all know, is about bolts. Bolts are fine. They make safe, enjoyable routes in places that would otherwise be ignored. They have no place on traditional crags, but on limestone and slate they make sense. The practice of retro bolting is more dubious, but again makes a certain amount of sense in certain places.

Chalk

For the vast majority of rock climbers in England and Wales the use of chalk is no longer an issue: it is used by the majority of climbers on the majority of routes. It is likely that the first piece of equipment a climber will buy today is a chalk bag as most youngsters start climbing on indoor walls. It is not so long ago that the use of chalk was a major issue and there are still a good number of climbers who decline to use the stuff and a small number who actively try to stop people using it.

Why? Well, the reasons are fairly simple. At first the argument centred around the use of chalk as a means of aid; this argument does not really hold water as chalk doesn't make the moves any easier, but just stops one from greasing off the holds. A more substantive argument against chalk is the offence it might cause to non-climbers, the argument being that the general public do not wish to see crags covered in the white stuff when out for a Sunday walk. I can to a certain extent sympathize with this. The chalk will, however, wash away, and doesn't do any lasting harm to the crag. I also believe that the majority of people are not offended by chalk on the crags; at any rate, I have never heard anyone complain. The third criticism of the use of chalk, and a more immediate one from a climber's point of view, is that chalk all over the holds will show the next climber the way to go and thus spoil his on-sight challenge. Again, I can sympathize with this point of view but rarely hear people complaining. It seems to me that using chalk is all right, but that maybe we should try not to throw it around too much.

Chipping

I would have thought that this was not an issue, that chipping is totally out of order and goes right against what climbing is about. Others may not agree, suggesting that utterly blank pieces of rock should be chipped to make a route. I cannot agree with this; the point of climbing is surely to accept the natural challenge and use whatever holds are available to climb a particular piece of rock. If there aren't any then leave it alone.

Cleaning

The practice of cleaning routes has been going on for a long time now. Very few new routes are climbed on sight; most are cleaned and inspected first. Cleaning takes several forms; brushing I feel is OK up to a point, that point being where excessive wire brushing leaves the rock looking scarred and previously blank rock develops indentations. The practice of removing loose rock is also all right, but again up to a point, the point being chipping. Paul Williams tries to justify chipping on the Colossus Wall by saying that it's a man-made quarry anyway. So is Millstone Edge, but I doubt if he would advocate doing the same thing there.

Removing large amounts of vegetation is also less acceptable in these ecologically minded days. About this I find it hard to make a decision, but I do disagree with the removal of trees.

Pegs

Since the advent of bolts, pegs have ceased to be an issue. In fact it has been a long while since they were an issue. Before the Second World War they were the scourge of British climbing, a foreign import that we did not want here, much the same as bolts were in the 1980s. The Munich climb was an example of foreigners using pegs and was thus

You need to be strong to climb at the highest levels: Sean Myles' back.

highly controversial. However, by the 1950s, as has happened today with bolts, the leading activists were merrily whacking in the pegs. The difference was, I assume, that pegs actually went into natural features, rather than having to have a hole drilled to accommodate them. If it were not for the repeated insertion and removal of pegs, London Wall would never have existed, so they have done some good. *In situ* pegs on sea cliffs are a menace, however, and more often than not a horrible rusty streak is left where they were once situated. I suppose this is all rather old hat, but it would be nice to see the use of pegs kept to a minimum.

New Routes

The style and manner in which new routes are ascended and the claims of people to have done routes that they plainly haven't, are areas of great controversy. Basically, to claim a new route one should have either flashed it or redpointed it. This ethic, drawn from sports-climbing, may call into question many first ascent claims. In certain areas, and I am thinking specifically of Gogarth, the ethic is very much to do new routes on sight. There are fewer and fewer possibilities for the bold climbers among us and I fully agree with those who maintain that areas such as Gogarth should be left for this style of ascent.

Along with the bolt has come the project. Here a very strong ethic prevails. A climber who has cleaned a piece of rock and then invested even more time and a not inconsiderable amount of money in equipping that route does not then want to see some other person nip in and get all the glory of the first ascent. It is usual, therefore, to leave a project for the person who has equipped it, even if he is not capable of the route and may have to work it for a great period. This may seem strange to the more traditional climbers among us who are used to a more competitive scene, where anyone who could, would get in and do the first ascent. It is because of this attitude that such unusual events happen as those witnessed at Kilnsey in 1991. A climber had cleaned and equipped a line and was working at it, but was unable to put it all together. A visiting climber asked if he could have a go and got very close to doing the route. He wanted another go. The first climber, realizing that his project was about to be nicked, said, 'no'. There was a confrontation. The first climber then ascended the route and on the abseil covered some of the holds with grease and removed some of the bolts, so that no one else could try it.

These are strange times in which we live.

Style of Ascent

There are many different ways of ascending a route. In order of moral superiority they are:

1. Soloing the route, on sight, naked.
2. More realistically, soloing the route, again on sight.
3. For the more ordinary and sane, climbing the route with the safety of a rope, protection, chalk, sticky boots and so on, but on sight without falling off, that is, *on-sight flash*.
4. Then comes the humble *flash*, that is, climbing the route with prior knowledge but without falling off.
5. Climbing the route on sight with rests and other aids doesn't really count.
6. The last acceptable form of ascent is the *redpoint*. That is where you may have tried a route, failed to climb it in practice, built a model of it in your garden to practise on, and then after much hard work, you eventually climb the route from the bottom to the top without falling off.

Anything else is dubious, although on some routes just getting to the top no matter how is quite enough.

The Devil's Slide, Lundy

The important thing is to be honest. Can you really live with yourself if you have claimed to have done routes that you haven't? I certainly couldn't.

CLIMBING – A LIFE PHILOSOPHY

We were driving back down the M1 after a weekend's climbing in the Peak District. It had been Peter's first introduction to grit and he had ticked off a few classics and enjoyed himself immensely in the process. Chequers Buttress, Three Pebble Slab, Bond Street one day and Amazon Crack and Boney Moroney the next. In between there had been a visit to the Grindleford Café, where he had been so amazed at me eating a full breakfast that he had had to take a photograph – they do not have that sort of food in Germany – and a wild firework party in Winster.

The journey back to London is always long and boring, and this one looked like being the same until Peter asked me an unusual question: 'What is your life philosophy of climbing?'

This was not an easy question to answer, particularly as I did not know what he meant by 'a life philosophy'. As we talked it over, however, I began to understand and found that indeed I did have a strong life philosophy of climbing.

What I mean by this is not simply an insight into why we climb, but what climbing gives us that makes us want to climb more and be involved in climbing. Why do we live a 'climbing lifestyle'? We have probably all heard of the 'fitness lifestyle', a philosophy that says 'I choose to be physically active, to arrange my life around my desire to stay fit and healthy, and everything else in my life is subordinate to staying fit.' This style of living is becoming increasingly popular in our society to a greater or lesser extent. Few take it to the extreme of the professional bodybuilder who does nothing except train, eat and sleep; most people are aware that they should take some form of exercise and endeavour to do so. Unfortunately most people's efforts are in vain as

Bouldering at the Bowderstone. Climber: Sean Myles

they do not have the discipline to maximize their potential.

It is the same with climbing. Visit any climbing wall and there are generally more people standing around at the bottom chatting than getting on with systematic training. Their trips to the wall will have some benefit, in the sense that it is probably better to do some training than none at all, but they will not progress as they would if they were more disciplined and organized. However, I am straying from the point, which is not how to organize your physical training.

My life philosophy of climbing covers more than just one thing but is inextricably linked with the reasons for climbing.

Climbing is a physical activity. This is stating the obvious, I know, but it is physical in several dimensions. I like the feelings in my body when I am climbing, I like the sensations of the muscles contracting and stretching, the feeling of movement, the dynamism. I like the feeling of power, the flexing of my joints, the contorted positions involved in climbing a piece of rock. I like the feeling of my muscles pumping, fingers uncurling, of keeping the power on just long enough. I like the ache after I have climbed. My body feels alive, it feels fit, it feels good, it feels like it has been used for a purpose.

Rock climbing is a tactile experience. The feel of different types of rock and of different holds adds to my pleasure and is something I would miss if I was unable to climb. The difference between the quarried gritstone of Millstone Edge, hard and rough, and the warmer feel of natural grit, the difference between gritstone and limestone, the difference between polished and unpolished limestone on the same crag, the different feel of holds on the same route and the different feel of the same hold on different days all add to the fascination of climbing. One day the holds are hot and sweaty, another day dry and full of friction. The feeling of jamming, of pinching, of undercutting, all are different and all have their place. The joyous feeling when a good hold is unexpectedly found is incomparable.

Mind control plays a large part, whether it is control of fear, the need to concentrate the mind to work out a move, to use the mind to control the body, to find protection, to be dedicated enough to try a problem repeatedly until it is successful, to keep on training; all need a strong mental control. The feeling of being scared, of not wanting to be in a situation, yet controlling that fear, forcing yourself to be calm and getting out of that situation under your own steam, that is a fine sensation. To succeed eventually on a problem that once seemed impossible and then only a distant possibility is elating.

Emotions. Climbing gives highs and lows, along with success or failure. It teaches one about oneself. The realization that one does not have what it takes to do a climb, accepting that and coming to terms with it, is an important lesson. Climbing will find out your strengths and weaknesses like no other sport. There is no opponent or referee to hide your own failings behind, just you. The elation of completing a long sought-after route, and the joy of the situations that come with climbing are all without par.

The environment. Climbing takes you to places unvisited by ordinary people: the bottom of a sea cliff reached only by abseil, or a mountain crag off the beaten track. It brings you closer to nature. Your interaction with the rock and the natural environment opens up new avenues of awareness. Wild flowers, rare birds, magnificent skies – all are part of the life of the climber.

Competition. Climbing is by its nature competitive, but in the most egalitarian of ways. Organized competitions have made climbing more competitive in a standard way, but this is a healthy channel for that instinct. Competition with yourself is more common, that constant striving for improvement.

I also feel part of a community. When I meet another climber we immediately have a point of contact. We have a vocabulary of our own which leads to communication. We all have a shared experience, an experience we can only share with other climbers.

Climbing is anarchic in that it has no rules, only ethics and even these are constantly changing. They are enforced by individuals on themselves, a form of self-restraint. Other people do not understand climbing and this again is part of the attraction, a striving for individualism.

This, briefly, is my philosophy, if you can call it that. It is my answer to Peter's question. I have written it for you in a spirit of honesty, and I hope it helps you to understand your motivation.

The Routes

PART 1
THE SOUTH AND WEST

—— 1 ——

INFIDEL

Infidel who with thy finite wisdom
Wouldst grasp things infinite and dost become
A scoffer of God's holiest mysteries;
Behold this rock then tremble and rejoice
Tremble for he who form'd the mighty mafs
Could in his justice crush thee where thou art
Rejoice! – that still his mercy spares thee.

J.H. PHIPPEN, 21 March 1831

Thus reads the inscription carved into the warning rock, at the home of the centrepiece of High Rocks climbing, Infidel.

Sustained 6a climbing from the safety of a top rope is the order of the day. First climbed and later soloed by Mick Fowler, the route is hard to start and even harder to keep moving on. The crux, if there is only one (and I think there are more), is rocking over on the break in the middle. Reaching the break is hard and getting off it is hard too, so be prepared for a long battle if you are to rejoice and not be crushed where thou art.

Infidel. Climber: Steve Gorton.

—— 2 ——

KRAITE ARETE

The crux rockover.

The finest product of a great climber. Kraite Arete was first climbed by Martin Boysen, one of that increasingly rare breed, a climber who is able to perform at a high standard on rock as well as in the mountains.

The route follows an obvious arete and is technical in the extreme: not powerful, not sustained, but a route where technique is everything. So much so that one day, now written into sandstone history, a bet was made. The bet was simple, that a well-known Sheffield climber and member of the British competition team could not flash the route on sight. The reward was fifteen pints.

The crowd gathered below and the climber started out in complete silence. He passed the crux, a fiendish rock over on a smear moving from one side of the arete to the other, then cruised up the arete. Nearing the top, the hard climbing over, he inquired as to where the finishing holds were as he could not see them. The air was not disturbed by even the quietest of hints. 'Oh, come on lads' the climber pleaded, but to no avail.

Needless to say he completed the route but received just one pint for his trouble. He is still waiting for the other fourteen.

Cruising up the arete, with the High Rocks Inn in the background. Climber: Matt Smith.

— 3 —

SECOND GENERATION

*A figure of four leads to a
one-finger pocket.
Climber: Jas Sharpe.*

*Looking round for the crucial
but hidden finishing holds.*

It is an ill wind that blows no one any good. So it was with the great storm of 1987. Everyone remembers where they were that night and the devastation the next morning. It wasn't just days, weeks or months before the mess was cleared up, it was years. The effects are still with us today.

Sussex and Kent were two of the worst-affected areas. After the storm you couldn't get to Harrison's Rocks because of the number of trees covering the path. It wasn't all bad news, however. Over at High Rocks the loss of certain trees allowed some always damp rock to dry out properly for the first time. It took a little longer for anyone to capitalize on this, then in the summer of 1991 a super-enthusiastic youngster called Jasper Sharpe managed to climb what is probably the best route on sandstone.

The route takes the arete of a formerly aided prow. The old bolts were removed – simply pulled out by hand – the line was cleaned and battle commenced.

The route is long for southern sandstone, being about 45ft, and combines a series of very technical sections. First you go up thin flake undercuts to a break, then you lock a toe in the break and reach up for another smaller break, figure of four on this break to a finger pocket, then teeter up the final blunt prow with the holds hidden from sight around to the left.

It is a magnificent route, the beauty of which can be viewed from a comfortable seat on an old tree trunk below. This is the very tree whose death made the climb possible.

4

AVERNUS

In the back of the cave of Avernus. Climber: Mike Eden.

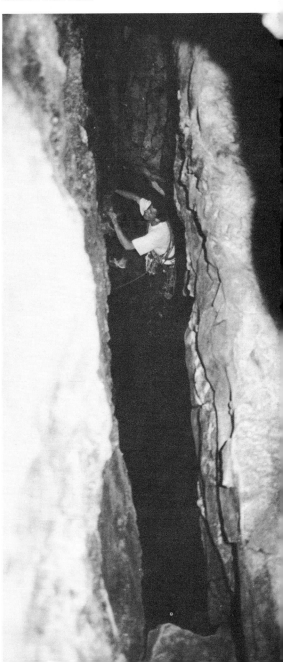

Climbing is full of surprises. The unexpected loose hold. The unexpected lack of protection. A fulmar dive-bombing you. A jug appearing from nowhere just as you are about to pump and fall off. Routes which are hidden away but brilliant.

Avernus is such a climb, a surprising route in many ways. Once it has been found, around the corner of the pedestal from the main part of Swanage's Subliminal cliff, the climber will be confronted by either a queue or no one at all. This depends mainly on the weather: on a hot, sunny summer's day the crowds will be queuing to gain some relief from the heat. On a misty grey day the cave will be deserted, the sea crashing in, making the approach more difficult and the starting ledges at the back damp.

The route starts up the ledges at the back of the cave and traverses out across the roof, but luckily there is a slot running the length of the roof that provides foot and hand holds and good protection. This is a fantastic position for the grade. You can look down between your legs and see the waves breaking into the cave on the boulders at the bottom. The route then tops out through a hole in the top of the cliff where you emerge mole-like into the sunlight, to rejoin the usual crowd at the top of Subliminal.

Belaying at the top of the route. Climber: Mike Eden.

—— 5 ——

FINALE GROOVE

Climbing at Swanage is full of contrasts and surprises. A day with howling winds at the cliff top will be too warm on the route itself. Between sections of loose rock there will be magnificent sections of solid limestone. Steep lines up impressive sections of the cliffs will go at surprisingly easy grades. Nowhere is this more the case than the central section of Boulder Ruckle.

Looking west from below the lighthouse above the Black Zawn there is one really obvious feature along the miles of cliff. Marmalota Buttress is the point of entry to the Ruckle. A somewhat scary 140-ft free abseil leads past loose blocks and intimidating ground to the sea-level boulders. It is here that the seriousness of climbing in the Ruckle will become shockingly real. There is just no obvious easy way out. The cliffs stretch unbroken in either direction, the sea crashes against the boulders behind. You're committed now.

A scramble westwards leads past the incredible hanging corner of Buccaneer to the less steep but no less inspiring corner of Finale Groove. From the bottom it looks all right. There appear to be plenty of holds and plenty of runner placements, and the angle doesn't look too bad either. The initial wall passes, proving maybe more problematical than expected, until the safety of a huge thread is reached. Now comes the crux. Here the corner juts out above your head and it is necessary to step up and left, out over space, to the continuation of the wall. The holds are big but it is strenuous, the thought of failure and a fall taking you crashing back into the corner is ever present. The exposure out there above the sea and the boulders plays on your mind. Then the moves are past and the runners sorted. It is here that the route really gets going. What looks from

Below the crux of Finale Groove. Climber: Ray Tipton.

below as if it will be easy climbing turns out to be continuously pumpy, as each move up doesn't lead to a rest. Runners are placed in the face of an ever-increasing pump. Eventually the climbing eases and the freedom of the cliff top is reached, where you can lie in peace looking at the sea, trying to psyche yourself up to go back down.

—— 6 ——

OCEAN BOULEVARD

Boulder Ruckle is synonymous with steep strenuous routes. There are many, at all grades.
Boulder Ruckle is also synonymous with loose
rock, also on routes of all grades. Happily the far
western section of Boulder Ruckle is steep but not
loose.

Locating the top of the routes is always difficult, so when you have found the abseil into this
section of the cliff take a deep breath. Having
descended the grass to the cliff edge, it suddenly
drops away from you – this is the line of Ocean
Boulevard. Spinning slowly down on the rope
one can appreciate just how steep the wall is, and
this isn't even the steepest part.

The route itself takes an obvious line, but
before you start, check out the other lines such as
Wall of the Worlds and Mother Africa, as they are
worth coming back for.

Ocean Boulevard follows a steep crack to an
overlap. The climbing is steep from the start but
surprisingly easy on big holds, the crack absorb-
ing gear at regular intervals. A rest of sorts can be
had below the overlap, passing which proves to
be the crux. Once past this, the angle, if not the
climbing, eases and it is one tired pair of arms that
will pull you over the top for a well-earned rest in
the long grass.

Ocean Boulevard.

—— 7 ——

LEAN MACHINE

Steep, sustained, strenuous and superb are adjectives used in abundance in the Swanage guide, and all of these apply to Lean Machine.

The far western part of Boulder Ruckle, approached by abseil or a boulder hop from Ocean Boulevard, is even steeper than Ocean Boulevard. It is not a place for anyone with a lack of forearm stamina, or 'umph' in the shoulders.

The route follows a discontinuous crack line up a superb white wall. By halfway the forearms are pumping and it is here that the angle starts to increase. As the angle increases the climbing gets harder and the crux, a move rightward, will see the unfit take to the air.

It is not all over there, as the angle doesn't ease and the arms scream for relief. It is now that many will have to make the climber's most difficult decision – whether to keep moving and try to get to the top before tiring completely, or to stop and put gear in, but then be too tired to get to the top and consequently fall off! Of course it is never certain that a fall will be avoided by not putting gear in, so it is better to put it in because, as we all know, pride goes before a fall.

Getting to the top of the wall Swanage's Achilles heel rears its ugly head: loose rock! The rock is actually not too bad so long as it is treated with care, which is not always easy when you're knackered. As the forearms slowly unpump, the route can be appreciated in full for what it is: steep, sustained, strenuous and superb.

The leaning wall of Lean Machine, showing the angle of the route. Climbers: Pete Oxley and Mike Eden.

——— 8 ———

POLARIS

Swanage has many different characters – the steep, sustained pumps of Boulder Ruckle, the carefree solos of Fisherman's West, the introductory routes of Subliminal and Cattle Troughs, the huge roofs of Laughing Arthur (the longest free roof in Britain) and Mind Cathedral, and what Swanage is best known for, namely big, scary, committing routes that are maybe best savoured on completion.

Polaris, just west of Blackers Hole (home of Laughing Arthur), is a brilliant test of commitment and keeping it together. The route follows an undercut arete with a traverse on a slab into a completely bottomless overhanging groove. There are no boulders at the bottom on which to belay, there is nowhere to lower off to in case of failure and the angle of the rock means it is impossible to reach an *in situ* ab rope!

To reach the bottom of the climb and get to the arete, one must abseil about 100 feet to the west to a boulder. This is often sea-washed, in which case a hanging belay is taken. It is apparent that the tides have little effect on the routes at Swanage, they are generally affected more by the swell, so check this. From here a long traverse on slightly suspect rock leads to the arete and a belay. The next pitch, and the technical crux, traverses a very exposed slab to reach the groove, which is followed by superb climbing in an incredible position to the grass at the top.

Polaris is an incredibly isolated position, and the feeling of isolation is multiplied on the route. The advantage is that you know what's coming. Did the first ascensionists?

Polaris. The route traverses in from the left for 100ft then follows the arete until the small slab is crossed and the upper groove ascended.

—— 9 ——

CONGER

Fisherman's West, a different and less well-known section of the Swanage cliffs, is popular with a certain band of Swanage climbers – those who like jumping into the sea from a great height. Forget bridge jumping or bobbing, make yourself a parachute out of a sheet of plastic, some string and bits of broom handle, then leap into the void!

Fisherman's West also has some of the cleanest, most solid rock at Swanage. An affinity with the water being an advantage as the best routes, Freeborn Man and Conger, are best soloed on a hot sunny day, when a fall into the sea will prove a relief rather than a penalty.

Nearing the top of the route. Climber: Dominic Cook.

The route traverses out across clean rock undercut by an incredibly coloured clear sea. About half way across, hard moves are made by the rusting remains of an old aid peg, into a bottomless chimney above a sea cave. This is the most popular place from which to take a plunge as it's only about thirty feet from the water! After being successful on this part keep it together; the further up the route, the further the distance is to fall back down into the sea – surprise, surprise! At the top the rock is solid and there is no grass slope, a relief especially when soloing. Having done the route without getting wet, it is best to take the plunge and jump from the top of the cliff, just to cool off.

— 10 —

CORONATION STREET

High Rock, Cheddar. Coronation Street takes the corner crack before crossing the obvious shield into the upper corner.

The most famous climb in the South West, product of the most famous British climber, named after Britain's most popular TV programme, subject of one of the most famous pieces of rock-related writing: but is it any good?

It's impressive, almost 400ft of near-vertical limestone towering above the car-park. It is also uninviting; the route starts up a long crack, it is cold and damp-looking, but it soon gets you high above the cars. After the second pitch the route trends slightly left through roofs and gets technically harder. Eventually the most famous and photographed part of the climb, the Shield, is reached. This is a jutting piece of rock that guards a leftward traverse to join an overhanging chimney. The situation is nerve-tingling, hand traversing 200ft above the ground. Above, the route becomes more strenuous before finally relenting, to give an easy 4c pitch to the top.

Speed is going to be a prerequisite for an ascent of Coronation Street. Not only is the route long but it has to be climbed in winter because there are too many tourists about in the Cheddar Gorge in the summer and the cliffs here are, well, just a little bit loose. Once back at the car, safe and warm, one can reflect on a route well done.

—— 11 ——

BIRD OF PARADISE

Cheddar Gorge contains a mass of rock which is gradually being taken over by the ivy, creating the new Hanging Gardens of Somerset.

Climbing here has lagged behind the rest of the country, partly because of seasonal restriction and partly because of lack of enthusiasts. Martin Crocker has been fighting the ivy, the cold and the apathy and has produced a number of very fine hard routes, which, if they were elsewhere, would receive the attention they deserve.

Bird of Paradise takes an awesome line of stepped roofs on Sunset Buttress. Originally an aid route, it has become a masterpiece of free climbing. Two E6 6b pitches sustain the interest, the second with *in situ* protection. Just getting to the start of the climb is an expedition in itself, but once at the start of the route the effort will appear to have been rewarded. The crux of the first pitch is a big roof, thankfully protected by a lone bolt. Overcome the roof and keep moving to a belay.

The second pitch is more sustained and technical, following the leftward line of roofs. This is strictly space-walking until a bottomless groove is reached. You're right 'out there', man, with space between your feet. If this was in the Peaks it would be mega-popular, but down in sleepy Somerset . . .

Sunset on Sunset Buttress. Bird of Paradise takes the left-hand line of roofs.

—— 12 ——

EMPIRE OF THE SUN

Torbay, the English Riviera. Anstey's Cove, the English Calanque.

How do these assertions stack up? Well, the climbing at Anstey's is as much like climbing in the Calanque as Torbay is like the French Riviera. Not that it's bad, rather it's similar but different.

There's a lot less of it and the routes are generally shorter, but there is a beach and a most beautiful cove and the rock is limestone. When it's sunny it's hot, just like in France. Too hot to climb, which is where the beach comes into its own.

Empire of the Sun is perched some way above the beach and on a sunny afternoon can be boiling hot. The rock, unlike some of the rock around, is good. The protection, after a runout to the first piece, is a friend 3 in a horizontal break and is good. The climbing between parallel horizontal breaks is superb. The route is not often flashed, and is strange in that a second attempt may feel easy and will usually result in success. This leads to controversy about the grade, and opinions vary between E5 6a and E6 6b, E6 6a being the popular and probably most correct version.

Anstey's is a nice place for a trip, a visit to Torbay in the evening being compulsory.

On the upper part of Empire of the Sun. Climber: Ian Vincent.

--- 13 ---

CIDER SOAK

Anstey's Cove in south Devon is a relatively new addition to the tour of British crags. On first sight it is easy to see why. The rock here is either very steep or looks like choss.

The cleanest wall is the Cider Soak wall which is home to a number of bolt-protected 'sports' routes. The angle is quite incredible. The routes look very short until you stand at the start and find the end of the route is 20–30ft behind your head. The routes also look chipped, but with Cider Soak this is not the case.

Cider Soak is about moves and the ability of the climber to link them. The moves are all interesting and the route as a whole, because of its angle and the small holds, is very strenuous indeed. It is the sort of route that will take some working and then will still not be easy to link. Desperate pulls, wild laybacks and bizarre horizontal contortions lead up the wall. The crux, when you are running out of steam, is near the top, hence its E7 grade.

Anstey's is a nice place for the job, however. There is the beach and the café, places to rest in between attempts and to relax. The relaxation possibly aids an ascent, while the consumption of too much rough cider in the evening, or too many cakes in the coffee shops of Biddecombe in the morning, will have the opposite effect.

One of many powerful moves.
Climber: Dave Thomas.

—— 14 ——

SUSPENSION FLAKE

The delights of Hounds Tor are not readily apparent to the passing climber, who will usually head for the larger and more obvious Hay Tor. It looks small and a bit scrappy, and on closer inspection the rock doesn't look too great either.

But it is here at Hounds Tor, within sight of its more famous neighbour, that the most excellent micro VS can be found, in the form of Suspension Flake.

Best savoured on a warm, still summer evening, when sounds travel for miles across the moors and there is peace in the beauty of

the place, Suspension Flake makes a detour from the popular flow a more than worthwhile diversion.

As its name suggests, the route follows a huge flake, suspended in mid-air on the side of one of the many blocks that form the Tor. The climb is short but packs its punches right from the start, the initial moves up to gain the flake proving problematic. Heel-hooking and monkeying along the flake lead out into space until vertical climbing leads back up to the top, where the climber has to ask how such a short route can be so exposed. Are there any more like it lurking in such lesser known places?

Suspension Flake. Climber: Liz Clare

15

SACRÉ COEUR

Blackchurch Rock. Sacré Coeur climbs the centre of the seaward face.

Open most people's bum bags and the last thing you would expect to find is a set of tide tables. For climbers it is essential kit, along with white tape and nail scissors. If you actually work out how to use the tide tables correctly you will avoid the necessity of sitting on the beach at Blackchurch waiting for the tide to go out. Access to Blackchurch Rock can only be gained a couple of hours either side of low tide. 'It's a long way to go for just one route', was the comment of one climber we met in the pub, although even he said it was worth it.

Blackchurch has an atmosphere all of its own: dark, imposing, mysterious. The evening light has a pale haunting quality, the cliffs are dark and gothic, and the innocent fields and trees suddenly drop down into the sea. The atmosphere is heightened by the ruined lime kilns, the crumbling rock and the constant march of the waves breaking on the shore.

Sacré Coeur takes a crack line to the left of the centre of the seaward-facing slab of Blackchurch Rock. The slab looks smooth and holdless. It isn't the crack that provides holds for both hand and foot and a home for wires. Often wet lower down, the start can feel precarious, a difficult high step and move left is made after 20ft into the main crack. The climbing is now enjoyable, and the crack is followed until it peters out and thinner cracks lead to the top of the rock. The climbing is, and I quote Pat Littlejohn, 'pure delight'.

A scramble down the looser material at the back of the rock is made to the beach below the intimidating main cliff. Walking back through the woods to the car-park care should be taken. One wrong turn and the rest of the day will be spent walking around in circles trying to find a way back to the car. I know, I've done it.

Sacré Coeur. Climber: Fiona Lloyd.

—— 16 ——

FAY

You're in the right place when the tracker dishes can be seen on top of the cliff. The slope below reveals nothing until you look over and see the now legendary fins sticking out. They look so thin that you would think they would collapse if someone was to climb them, but they don't. Really!

The first fin arrived at, after scrambling down the muddy descent, is the north fin. Of course there are climbs on both sides of the fins; the south face of the middle fin has a concentration of excellent routes, the best being Fay.

The rock looks as though it is going to provide rounded holds and poor protection. Once started the opposite is found to be the case: all the holds

High on Fay. Climber: Dave Kendall.

The radar station above Lower Sharpnose.

feel like jugs, and although the climbing is very sustained and the angle steep, it is possible to shake out in many places.

Fay is about being fit. Taking the central line of the wall at its highest point, there are no particularly hard moves but an awful lot of climbing on steep rock. Opinion as to the grade varies between E5 6a and E4 6a depending on how fit you are; the biggest problem is holding on long enough to get the gear in. The trick is to put the gear in where you can rest and do the moves in between quickly.

The belay on top of the fin and the abseil back down again is quite freaky, and could prove to be more traumatic than actually climbing the route!

—— 17 ——

EROICA

To stumble on a cliff as smooth, clean and impressive as Pentire would be a dream for many climbers. For Pat Littlejohn, finding big cliffs and then climbing the best routes on them is a matter of course.

Pentire is one of the most impressive cliffs in Cornwall. Amongst a jumble of grass slopes, broken rocks, caves and coves, the great wall of Pentire stands out, smooth and grey, the top of the cliff a series of overhanging grooves, giving the climbs their twin aspects.

To the left of the wall is a line of cracks leading to a huge flake, the line of the first pitch of Eroica. The route then follows the central overhanging groove. The first pitch could be climbed by itself with a lower-off, at a standard of E1 5a but this would be missing the point. The first pitch does provide delightful climbing, passing two small overhangs and culminating in a layback up a massive flake.

The second pitch provides the kick in the tail. Hard moves (past the remains of a peg that used to provide aid) lead into the groove, which is then followed steeply to the top. The old option of climbing the route with aid has disappeared along with the peg, so it's a 6a move you'll have to make now. What a route, and this is the easiest on the face.

The huge flake of Eroica. Climber: Steve Anson.

—— 18 ——

DARKINBAD THE BRIGHTDAYLER

The traverse. Climber: Steve Anson.

In contrast to Eroica, its near neighbour, Darkinbad consists of technical and bold face climbing up the centre of this most dark and imposing of cliffs. The start is not so hard but requires a certain cool. The holds are flat, or sometimes sloping and the first protection is not reached until about 25ft. With the confidence given by the implied security of a runner, the climber can continue up to the left of a small roof and then traverse up and left following a line of cracks across the middle of the face past an old peg – a possible lower-off for those that are finding the going too tough – to a set of overhangs. The overhangs are passed via cracks to a stance in common with Eroica. The two routes cross at this point, Darkinbad taking the left-hand groove in the upper section of the cliff. The exposure is great here, the platform and sea far below between your legs, the groove rearing up before you, pushing you out.

Darkinbad isn't the only hard route at Pentire but it remains the best, and a tribute to Pat Littlejohn, who had the vision to climb the route, admittedly with aid, thus showing what would later be possible on this magnificent cliff.

—— 19 ——

DOORPOST

There used to be one compact guidebook covering West Penwith. It was of a manageable size and contained as much information as was needed. Granted some of the grading was a bit off, but the principle was right: small, manageable and compact. A replacement was needed but what has happened? There are now going to be two guidebooks, both bigger than the previous single one. To climb in West Penwith it will now cost twice as much in guidebooks alone. The current obsession with making guides bigger and more expensive has got to ridiculous proportions. They are rapidly becoming useless for their intended purpose, because of their sheer bulk and cost.

Contained in the Bosigran guide are two marvellous cliffs, Bosigran itself and the Great Zawn. Doorpost takes an obvious line straight up the middle of the main part of Bosigran. The route, which can be climbed in three pitches, really has two contrasting parts. The first pitch takes a rightward rising traverse line up a slab. The climbing is on small holds, the protection may feel a little spaced but it is OK. From the comfort of a large ledge, twin cracks soar skyward. These cracks are followed until they become one. From here a rib leads upward in the same line as the cracks, getting progressively easier. Care needs to be taken to avoid getting the ropes jammed near the top, leaving your second to climb unprotected!

The route is superb in every way, it is a must for any climber and should not be missed.

The second pitch of Doorpost.

—— 20 ——

BLACK SLAB

'It will be gusting up to gale force eight' the coast-guard had told me in the morning. She wasn't wrong. I was standing at the stance at the top of Black Slab as Sabina climbed up toward me. The sea crashed in below sending sheets of spray into the air to be blown back in the wind. The water ran back down the slab below as the next wave came in. It had started raining, it was great! The weather hadn't been too good all week but we had decided to make the most of it. We'd left the others sitting around in the van drinking tea and moaning about the weather. 'It will be all right' I had said, but the self-perpetuating cycle of apathy, lethargy and boredom had set in and all they could think about was going home. Peter arrived on the stance. 'I'm sorry about the weather,' I said. 'Oh no, this is fun !' he replied.

That summed up the day and the route. It wasn't hard, it was very easy, but it was fun.

When we got to the Tinners Arms the landlord put our wet clothes in his drier. As we supped our pints of HSD we agreed that the others had missed out. Climbing isn't just about sunny days and dry warm rock but about getting out there and having an adventure, getting wet but enjoying the situations, the environment and the elements. Black Slab had given us all of these.

Cornwall is steeped in history.

Black Slab is in a superb and memorable setting for such an easy route.

Pulling on to the slab on a not altogether perfect day. Climber: Sabina Gutte.

—— 21 ——

DREAM LIBERATOR

'Paradise Wall is more committing than the Great Zawn,' we had been told. After a testing time on Dream and a far more complicated approach our opinion was that this was not the case. To get to Dream you have to walk to Bosigran, cross Commando Ridge, descend to another platform, abseil 80ft to another platform and then make a committing downward jump to the ledge below the Green Cormorant Face.

If, as was the case this day, the route is very damp, the feeling of commitment is somewhat heightened. The fact that the opinion was that the route was still excellent, even in such trying conditions, reinforces the general view that this is one of the greatest routes around.

Basically it's got everything going for it. The setting is fantastic; I defy anyone not to find the Cornish coast in general beautiful, and in particular the Great Zawn, which is both beautiful and threatening. The incredible blues of the sea contrasting with the orange red of the rock, the light outside the zawn with the darkness inside, stick in the mind. The route is committing: when the leader has reached the belay and the second is desperately trying to pull through the roof on to the slab on the first pitch, they just want to get to the top. The climbing itself is great, the moves are always interesting, thought is always needed, even when the belay edge is tantalizingly close around the corner. The gear is good but at times well spaced, and a fall from the slab would be quite nasty. The route weaves an intricate line up the seaward arete of the zawn. From the belay there are two choices: to follow the finish of the Dream around to the left, or the finish of the Liberator up cracks to the right. The Liberator finish is more popular, making the route more sustained, but the Dream finish is still good.

Whichever way you choose, the route will stay in your memory. It is a route which fully lives up to its name.

The slab on pitch one.
Climber: Rowland Edwards.

The top pitch of Dream.
Climber: Steve Anson.

SAXON

'It's a route with a real crux. Anyone who is just climbing HVS or E1 will certainly come to a sticking point', I was told. The earliest of a trio of excellent climbs at Carn Kenidjack, the others being Rock Dancer and Stormbringer, Saxon is the original and another product of the ever-active Pat Littlejohn. It is a popular climb, one friend of mine making a special visit from London just to climb it, such is its appeal.

Kenidjack differs from other crags in Cornwall in its geological composition. It is made of Kilas slate rather than the more usual and famous red granite that makes up the majority of the cliffs in West Penwith. If slate is rare down here then so are slabs, the climbs usually approaching vertical, although for a slab this one is pretty steep.

The route climbs to a ramp, which is followed until it can be exited to a niche. From here the steep wall is climbed until better holds arrive along with a slightly easier angled depression. Steeper moves again lead to a horizontal break. The leader now has a choice: whether to follow the break to the right, belay and climb the wall above, or go straight up. The traverse was the original way and is a most obvious line, providing excitement for both leader and second. Straight up is slightly harder but somehow less satisfying.

If the route has whetted your appetite then try Rock Dancer; it is only slightly harder and provides fine climbing.

The slab of Saxon. Climber: Mark Edwards.

—— 23 ——

LAST DANCER

The traffic streams back and forth on the A30 to Land's End – car-loads of tourists keen to get a view of this last outpost of mainland Britain before America.

As climbers, you do not have to pay to park at Land's End, a concession from the landowner, who realizes that the sight of climbers on the cliffs is an attraction greater than the Giant Galleon or the Death Slide. Climbers look oddly out of place, however, as they walk to the cliff, kitted out with rucksacks and ropes.

Land's End is different from any other sea cliff. The sea is never calm, and standing at the top the noise is quite incredible. The light is also some-how different, quite superb in the evenings as the sun goes down below the Longships Lighthouse. There is an incredible atmosphere here, whether climbing or just sitting on top of the cliff. There are some rather good climbs here, too. Unfortunately one of the best, Yankee Doodle, recently disappeared.

Heading north from the car-park the line of Last Dancer can be seen on a pinnacle at the sea-ward end of Dr Syntax's Head, a promontory jutting out to sea below the First and Last House. There are two possible ways of climbing Last Dancer. The first, which is the original and harder way, is to get down to sea level and make moves up a wall that is climbed at E4 6c if the *in situ* limpet is in the correct place. The limpet moves around and can make the move correspondingly harder! This leads to a crack and then to the second pitch. The second pitch moves out left then back right until the arete proper is reached. The alternative is to miss out the initial wall and just climb the second pitch. This does not detract from the route, as the initial moves, although they are the crux, are somewhat artificial in their nature.

Last Dancer. Climber: Mark Edwards.

You are quite likely to be photographed climbing Last Dancer, as the route is in full view of the milling tourists and is in a quite spectacular position. So wear your best tights and T-shirt.

—— 24 ——

STONE BOOM

It is a peculiar name to which I gave little thought until I was underneath the climb. Once looking up at the line of the route I realized why it had been so called. The route first climbs a corner then traverses a horizontal crack. The edge of the buttress of rock curves back to meet the corner. The whole represents the mast, boom and sail of a boat, made from stone.

The rock in the corner is a little friable yet the climbing is easy. The traverse is quite superb. It looks as if it is going to be absolutely desperate, the bottom lip of the crack looking rounded, only faint nobbles for the feet. Once committed, small positive holds are found in the crack: swing across on these and a large ledge is reached with a sigh of relief; it is not as hard as it looks (E1). A few slightly more technical moves lead to another

The 5c crux on the top pitch.
Climber: Dave Hauton.

large ledge where it is usual to belay. With double ropes the route can be climbed in one pitch, making it more sustained and more 'out there'. The second pitch is the harder, the hardest move on the route being a 5c pull off the belay ledge. The holds and gear soon improve but the climbing remains fingery to the top, a complete contrast to the first pitch.

Stone Boom should not be missed. It is like two climbs in one, the two pitches are so different, yet so good.

The traverse on pitch one. Climber: Dave Hauton.

—— 25 ——

INTER SPACE

The Paradise Wall of Carn Les Boel is one of the most dramatic yet unfrequented cliffs in West Penwith. The wall has a peculiar atmosphere, dark and foreboding, the proximity of Bosistow island making the crag feel claustrophobic. It is an atmosphere which can be suddenly broken by the arrival of playful seals, who at a second glance will have disappeared, leaving the climbers to solitude and their battle with the rock.

The wall is steep and is reached by abseil down the easiest route, Scabbard, an HVS that could provide an escape in an emergency. Inter Space, although not the most obvious line on the wall, provides the best climbing, but a word of warning: the climbs hereabouts do not get many ascents and can be dirty. If this doesn't bother you then the route will prove a treat. The climb starts up Scabbard then traverses across on to the wall proper. Moves between breaks are made, leading steadily upward to a final roof, the last part of the climb, topping out, proving the crux. The gear is OK but Paradise Wall is not a place for failure. It is a place to enjoy climbing in solitude, in the most wonderful natural surroundings, and has an atmosphere all of its own.

Paradise Wall. The climber is just starting Inter Space. Climbers: Steve Anson and Dave Hauton.

—— 26 ——

PEGASUS

'Chair Ladder's answer to Doorpost', says Pat Littlejohn in *South-West Climbs*. 'An outstanding route, not to be missed', says Pete O'Sullivan in the *West Penwith* guide. So why?

Pegasus starts at sea level and ends at the top of the cliff, under the coastguard lookout. Following an elegant line, the route takes in some very varied climbing before its best pitch, a slab high on the cliff in a marvellous position. The approach is an interesting adventure in itself and should not be undertaken too lightly. Traversing into the base of the cliff from Zawn Rinny, a jump must be made across a channel, through which the waves are constantly moving. If the sea is rough or the tide is coming in then care needs to be taken. After the jump are sea-washed platforms, safe you think, until a wave breaks on the rocks behind and you are showered with spray. An alternative approach in bad weather is to descend a gully below the coastguard lookout to a ledge halfway up the route. This is fine except it lacks the purity of a start from sea level.

The route starts up a corner, then overcomes a small roof to get to the halfway ledge, which is all quite exciting as the tide comes in and your second starts to worry about getting wet feet. From the ledge the route climbs a short wall to belay below a curving corner crack and slab. You are quite high now and the sea seems a long way below. This is the best pitch on the route; using small holds on the slab for your feet, with hands and protection in the corner crack, you work your way up and right to belay by a block. This pitch is almost too easy-angled, the rock pulling you forward off balance. Look down and you will see the sea below, either blue and calm reflecting the sun's rays, or grey and menacing with great waves pounding the base of the cliff far below, the red Cornish granite changing colour with the

The fine curving corner of Pegasus. Climbers: Sabina Gutte and Peter Menke.

changes in the weather. The route is not over yet, and the last pitch, although escapable, is technically harder. Then all of a sudden you are at the top, the cliff now out of sight below, the route just a memory.

Walk back to Porthgwarra in sunshine or be torn by the howling Atlantic winds, pick blackberries in one season or smell wild garlic in another. Whatever your experience, Pegasus will return to your thoughts time and time again.

—— 27 ——

TERRIER'S TOOTH

It was a misty Saturday in October when I first went to Chair Ladder. We had driven down from London on the Friday night taking the scenic route and stopping at the pub before ending up camping in the car-park at Treen in the small hours. Conditions were perhaps not ideal: the days were not long and sunny, the rock was not warm and golden. On the other side of the coin we had the place pretty much to ourselves and could have our pick of the brilliant routes here. First we climbed the south face direct. This was memorable in itself but we had time for more and the obvious climb to do was Terrier's Tooth.

It proved to be a slightly less straightforward proposition than I had imagined from the grade (VD). More than once I started up the vein in the bottom wall only to climb back down nervously with apologies to my patient friend who was holding the ropes. Once I adopted a more positive frame of mind the initial section passed without too much trouble. That was the crux over. What followed was delightful climbing up the gradually narrowing pillar until the superb final cracked slab.

There we were on the top of the Terrier's Tooth and it was pretty well dark. It then occurred to us that we didn't know how to get off the pinnacle and back to the top of the cliff. After trying more than one alternative we found ourselves back at our rucksacks and packing up to scamper back to the car and an evening in the Logan Rock Inn. What a great day it was!

The harbour at Porthgwarra, the parking place for Chair Ladder.

Terrier's Tooth, with climbers on every pitch and belay.

Climbers on the first and second pitches of Terrier's Tooth.

—— 28 ——

THE CULL

What seems like an age away, and a complete change in character from West Penwith, is the Lizard, which is less impressive but has fewer tourists, a café in a most spectacular position and a charm and beauty all of its own.

The cliffs form a jumble of zawns, cave walls and buttresses, the centrepiece of which is Bass Point.

The Cull takes the inspiring central crack line in the upper part of the wall. An abseil leads to a sea-level platform. From here flakes to the right of an obvious slanting corner are climbed to horizontal breaks before the meat of the route begins. The crack is followed with good protection and an ever-increasing pump. The situation is spectacular, right out on the edge of the world with the blue Atlantic swell rolling in below. A problematic section is reached just below the top; once this is passed, success is ensured, the pleasure of the route and the situation just a memory.

The Cull. Climber: Andy Popp.

—— 29 ——

ARUCARIA

Lundy has many fine and impressive rock features, all the more beautiful for the stuff they are made of. Granite contains the most incredible colours, and the character of the cliffs alters more than most as the rock changes from flaming red to sultry grey.

One of the most impressive cliffs and the last to be breached is the St John's Stone. Containing a number of huge groove lines with a large roof at the bottom, it was not until 1991 that the first route here was climbed by Nick White and Neil Foster.

Arucaria manages to get the climber established under the roof by means of a jammed nut

The amazing hanging beam of Arucaria. Climber: Nick White.

and a jumar. This leaves you hanging from a huge suspended beam of rock that stays in place without any apparent support. The route traverses this as it vibrates until desperately strenuous climbing leads up around the roof into a groove and a belay ledge. The second pitch is more technical E6 6c, but less body-wrecking than the first, climbing the elegant hanging groove above.

Even today in the ever more competitive climbing scene, where new routes are kept as prized projects, there are opportunities, if you look hard enough, to discover magnificent new routes such as Arucaria. It requires a different sort of effort, an adventurous approach, the patience to visit more far-flung places such as Lundy, but, as I'm sure Nick will tell you, it's worth it.

The second pitch groove. Climbers: Nick White and Neil Foster.

— 30 —

SATAN'S SLIP

Towards the north of the west coast of Lundy lies the incredible sheet of rock known as the Devil's Slide. The slide is home to two well-known routes. One takes the name of the slide itself and is graded Hard Severe. The finer of the two routes is also harder.

Satan's Slip E1 5a was only climbed nine years after its easier companion, yet is grades harder. In common with its easier companion the route is easy to start; in fact the bottom quarter of the

Looking down the magnificent sweep of Satan's Slip.

The Devil's Slide with climbers on Satan's Slip.

slab can be climbed almost anywhere, it is only after 150ft that the difficulties start. The moves are thin and the gear is well spaced. The thought of a slip down the rough granite slab is not pleasant. The pitch is a long one – 140ft. Above this the route finishes easily to the left. But to stay in character, and perhaps more satisfyingly, a direct finish can be made with slightly harder but better protected moves than on the main pitch.

A fantastic slab climb, a fantastic Lundy climb.

PART 2
WALES

—— 31 ——

STAR GATE

Abseil to the platform at the bottom of Brazen Buttress when the tide is in and the platform will feel small and too close to the sea. From here a scramble round to the right will lead to the foot of the impressive through cave and thence to the start of Star Gate.

At low tide the whole area below the buttress is exposed and the atmosphere is far less foreboding, providing the opportunity to walk around the boulders and rock pools to look at the routes with comparative ease. Mother Carey's is a small area but with several fine routes.

Mother Carey's Kitchen.

Star Gate is the first on the Space Face and is a cosmic trip, a black hole which will consume even the largest rack. The climbing is thuggy at the bottom but steady once the hanging groove is reached, enabling you to savour a difficult situation from a reasonable position. It is worth while splitting the route at the end of the rightward traverse, from where the full horror of the Space Face can be appreciated.

It is up to you to decide if the quote in the guidebook is right: 'Only the best route in the world?'

Well, probably.

Moving up to the stance at the end of the first pitch. Climber: Gary Wickham.

The route continues steeply on the second pitch. Climbers: Gary Wickham and Bill Whatley.

— 32 —

ROCK IDOL

Mother Carey's can be seen in its entirety from the buttress of the White Tower: the Space Face on the right, the through cave of Deep Space, the arete of Herod, the face of Brazen Buttress and then the mighty corner of Rock Idol.

Rock Idol is reminiscent of the HVSs at Swanage – big, steep and impressive – yet this route is somehow better. The corner, which is the line of the route, bulges and leans back over the climber's head. These obstacles are avoided by climbing the wall on the right. Vertical cracks in the rock give the face an unusual look, as if it had been attacked and scarred by acid. The rock feels solid enough, but recent large rockfalls here show that the cliff as a whole is not so solid. The vertical cracks provide large holds and consume gear. The climbing gets progressively harder as height is gained and the angle gets steeper.

Once on the top of the cliff, with your arms gradually reverting to their normal size and shape, the scenery can be enjoyed and thoughts can run on to Herod, or Brazen Buttress, or even Star Gate. There are so many!

The incredible corner of Rock Idol. Climber: Ray Castle.

—— 33 ——

THE BUTCHER

From the boulders at the bottom of St Govans the routes look smaller than they feel when you are actually on them, the Butcher maybe more than most. Right by the abseil point, in full view of the passing hordes, the Butcher takes the very obvious feature of the steep seaward arete and is worth doing for those who like to attract attention to themselves: every time a climber sets hand and foot on the Butcher, the climbers around stop to watch, and the tourists lining the cliff top point and marvel.

The line of the route looks fairly obvious and covered in good holds, not too much harder than the neighbouring E1s, and short.

It has a reputation, reinforced by the guidebooks' description of 'a meaty little pitch', for being a test piece. Well, if you are just starting to climb E3 then it is just that, testing strength, confidence and stamina. Stamina on an 80ft pitch? Well yes, because if you hang around trying to place gear or work out what to do, if you try to climb the crux static and in control, the route will require stamina. On the other hand, if you take a positive approach, cruise up the bottom wall, drop in some wires on the way, shake out on the jug then go for it, making a big lunge around the arete for a hidden jug, you'll be all right, swinging up to the top and the

Moving around the arete of the Butcher.

admiration of the passers-by and your fellow climbers.

It's a great little route, one you can't fail to get a buzz from.

TREVALLEN PILLAR

Trevallen is the closest crag to the car-park at St Govans Head but is not the most popular. The reason is simple – the routes here are generally hard, the majority being in the E4/E5 bracket.

Trevallen Pillar is one of the most popular and well-known routes here, having appeared on the cover of the guidebook. It has two highly contrasting pitches. The first is technical face climbing on small holds and perfect rock. The crux is a move out of a depression with the gear at foot height. It is easy to mess up first go but proves not so hard once worked out. This move leads toward the left-hand arete, bigger holds and a belay.

In contrast the second pitch has bigger holds, is steeper and is less well protected. It is this pitch that gives the route its E4 grade, a long reach for a sloping hold above gear with the possibility of hitting the belay ledge proving the most worrying move. The hard section up the arete is followed by a short steep wall to arrive at the top of the crag and meet the admiring crowds of tourists. It is only five minutes' walk from the car-park so be prepared to be watched as Trevallen Pillar is open to view from the cliff top. You will probably be asked if you go abseiling, and if you've got all the gear, it's that sort of place.

Moving on to the crux. Climber: Gary Wickham.

The crux 6a move right, on the first pitch of Trevallen Pillar. Climber: Gary Wickham.

The scary top arete proves the crux of the route. Climber: Gary Wickham.

—— 35 ——

PLEASURE DOME

Welcome to the Pleasure Dome. We're a long way from Xanadu. No, not the route in the Great Zawn but the mystic capital of Kubla Khan. The south Pembroke coast, Stennis Head, to be more precise, is the setting, at a nice crag with an easy scramble to the bottom and some good routes, like Manzouko and Cool for Cats. Pass these and around the corner will be found a bulging slab of white rock with a steep wall above. The slab is undercut, the sea coming right up to the bottom.

The route takes a curving fault line around the top of the slab. A large block is reached and the climb gets steeper and more strenuous. A groove is followed, the moves are hard and the angle isn't easy. The line is compulsive, the climbing sustained.

The traverse goes a long way before going up.
Climber: Ian MacIntyre.

The route gets steeper on the upper section.

To get on to the slab a very narrow zawn has to be crossed. It has been known for seconds to throw themselves down this to save their leaders. Rather them than me. The rock here, as in a lot of places in Pembroke, is sharp, hence part of the attraction of Pembroke climbing: super situations, good rock, good climbing and reasonable grades. Pleasure Dome has all these except that the grade is about right or maybe a little tough. Either way, it is still a Pleasure.

— 36 —

BLOODY SUNDAY

Huntsman's Leap is an incredible natural feature – a narrow zawn cutting a jagged gash into the fields that form the Castlemartin firing range on the south Pembroke coast. A short flat walk from the car-park and there it is. There is no warning, just this great hole in the ground, with two steep smooth walls. The West Wall is the better of the two – a steep, pink expanse of rock criss-crossed by fine routes. At the landward end of the wall is Bloody Sunday, one of the most popular routes in the Leap.

It is also a route of immense character and quality. After abbing into the zawn and experiencing that special, quiet, echoing atmosphere that is peculiar to this place, a start can be made on the route.

A steep bouldery wall to start. The rock is clean and smooth, as it is washed by the sea, and the moves are powerful. The route trends leftward until more broken ground is reached. The climbing difficulties ease but the protection is poorer. The crux of the route is high up. Moving rightward into a groove, you will be quite tired now, but keep it together. The groove is followed to the top, the wind, the crowds and the sheep.

Bloody Sunday is a great route in a great situation. Do it and enjoy it.

High on Bloody Sunday.

--- **37** ---

SOULS

Souls is a fine route taking a line up the centre of the pink West Wall of Huntsman's Leap. It breaks out right after the start of Witch Hunt and follows a line up a flake and wall above.

It is commonly regarded as *the* route of the leap, yet at E6 6b, a grade attained by many people these days, it gets few ascents. There is a good reason for this. The state of the *in situ* gear is appalling. What placements there are contain hammered-in hexes, which in the salty sea air have corroded so they are now just lumps of rust. The moves are committing and now that there isn't any gear they are dangerous too. It is the perfect illustration of the point made by many people, that *in situ* gear should not be used on sea cliffs. Resin bolts are a different matter, since if properly placed and sealed they do not corrode, but ordinary gear hammered in place and left to rot is not only unsightly but downright dangerous. So what should be done? Should a route as good as Souls undoubtedly is, be left unclimbed by all but those who are more willing to put their life on the line than the early ascensionists, or should the protection be replaced by something more permanent, that will not rot with the passage of time? Is it time to reconsider the 'no bolts in Pembroke' ethic? I do not have the answer, but it is an issue we should address.

Moving up the groove requires strong nerves, the in situ *gear having now corroded.*

—— 38 ——

LUCKY STRIKE

Pembroke at Easter can offer numerous and varied delights. These generally depend on the weather. It can be hot, sunny and near Mediterranean in climate, or wet, cold and windy, with the waves breaking not only at the bottom but also over the top of the cliffs.

Camping at the vicarage campsite can start off a pleasant experience, with a leisurely dinner cooked outside followed by a stroll over to St Govans. By the time the pub closes everything could have changed. By the next morning the campsite could have turned into a quagmire, vehicles slipping in the mud and the distinct chance of contracting trench-foot if you linger too long.

If things turn out well, the climbs will leave memories of sunny days and warm dry rock with good friction. If the conditions are the opposite the experience and memories will be different, but maybe reinforced by adversity.

Lucky Strike is a superb Pembroke route, taking a rising diagonal traversing line up what otherwise looks like a blank wall. It is situated in the corner of a bay, and even on calm days has a big-cliff feel. On a rough day it would be a wild, lonely and frightening place. The feeling of isolation is accentuated by the deserted radar station on the cliff top above.

The climbing may feel easy, and views range as to the grade, from HVS to E2: HVS for the climbing, E2 for the situation.

The rising traverse of Lucky Strike. Climber: Zoe Panchic.

—— 39 ——

PIGS ON THE WING

The sea is hundreds of feet below. There is a huge roof above. The rock is wet and it is approaching dark. Such is the experience that Pigs on the Wing has to offer.

It is a route for those with a certain degree of commitment, something that is lacking in a lot of us. The grade may sound fairly easy (HVS) but when you look at it and realize that there are three pitches and that if you fall off there is an overhang below as well as above, it makes you question your ability, or else you carry jumars. Even then a long fall will turn the climb into an epic experience. Once into the second pitch there is no rescue.

If you are cool then the situation will be massively enjoyable, if not it will be frightening. The weather will also play a part. OK, you're under a roof and should be sheltered from the rain, but with a bit of a wind blowing communication will not be too easy, and the rain will probably blow in from the sea, which will be crashing in below.

If it's an 'out there' experience you desire then this is the route for you.

Pigs on the Wing pitch two.
Climbers: Nigel Fawthrop and Bill Whatley.

—— 40 ——

AXLE ATTACK

Low on Axle Attack.

Once when staying in Dieniolen I was shown the axle that was reputedly used for training prior to the first ascent of Axle Attack – a heavy, rusty lump of iron from an old quarry truck. We used it to try to keep warm, by having exercise competitions, as there was no heating in the house. Whether it had anything to do with Axle Attack I do not know.

Thirty miles away at Llandudno is the marine drive and above it Pen Trwyn. It is here that after much negotiation with the authorities – resulting in bolt belays above the routes – we can once again climb Axle Attack.

The location of Axle Attack is obvious – a line of bolts marking the way up a wall of beautiful white limestone. The wall itself looks so good but is not as steep as one might have expected. The climb meanders in its lower half, zigzagging up the lower slabby wall. The angle then steadily increases, as does the difficulty of the climbing. The pump starts, the moves get harder until the crux, right at the top of the route, is completed or . . . back down for another attempt.

Axle Attack.

— 41 —

STATEMENT OF YOUTH

A route for the masses
Ben Pritchard, May 1991

I disputed this point with Ben and eventually we concluded that maybe twenty or twenty-five people had climbed Statement. It just shows that whatever grade you climb at you believe everyone else to be better.

Statement of Youth was first climbed by Ben Moon, who was seventeen at the time. It was a breakthrough in British climbing, being for a long time the most sustained, if not technically the hardest, British route. It was the first British route to use eight bolt runners. It showed the way forward in climbing, the way that standards would improve. The ultimates are harder now and there are few people that can climb them. The fact that so many people have now climbed Statement and probably 100-odd people in Britain alone have now climbed E7 and above shows how general standards have improved.

Why is Statement of Youth such a good route? Well, it is not just a clip up following nothing more than a line of bolts. It follows a natural line: you go up a steep wall to a roof, through the roof with a heel hook, then traverse leftwards until a line of undercuts leads strenuously back right to final delicate moves up a slabby groove to a welcome chain and lower-off. Phew! You've gotta be fit for this one.

A steep start leads to the famous heel-hook traverse.
Climber: Adam Wainwright.

An overhanging traverse leads back right to thin moves on the final wall.

The final flake of Statement of Youth.

Lowering off.

The angle of the route and the technicality of the climbing is sustained on Liquid Amber. Climber: Ben Moon.

—— 42 ——

LIQUID AMBER

The seaside town of Llandudno on the north Wales coast is not a typical place to find rock climbers. It doesn't exactly have a feeling of being wild and 'out there'. Walk down the High Street and pop into the record shop or the amusement arcade and you may spot any number of Britain's top climbers, however, attracted to Llandudno not for the entertainment of the town but for the entertainment of the Ormes, two lumps of limestone sticking into the sea on either side of Llandudno bay. The most popular is the Great Orme, and the most popular part of it is Lower Pen Trwyn. The crag, visible from the pier, can be reached in about ten minutes from the car-park.

LPT sports a series of very steep powerful sports' climbs on rock of the most excellent quality. It is the antithesis of North Stack, the climbs being bolt-protected and the crag approached from the bottom, the tops of the routes having lower-off chains.

Liquid Amber is one of a clutch of safe E9s to have been climbed in 1990, heralding the new decade with a jump in standards. Ben Moon's Hubble at Raven Tor is a short and desperate power problem, where just doing the moves is virtually impossible, let alone linking them. The Very Big and the Very Small on the Rainbow Slab is the ultimate in slab routes, tried for a very long time by Nick Harms and eventually climbed by Johnny Dawes. The route takes an amazing amount of concentration just to stay on, let alone move. Neither of these has had a second ascent. Liquid Amber, however, first climbed by Jerry Moffat, has been tackled again, by Ben Moon, who rated it as one of the best routes in the world. It is different again in style to the other two routes in that it is very steep and very sustained, the climbing being excellent all the way. It doesn't follow such an obvious line as Statement, but makes up for this with the quality of the climbing.

It isn't just sustained climbing at a reasonable technical grade, but sustained climbing with 7a moves. For you and me it may be difficult to comprehend what this means. Watching Ben on his first day on the route the moves looked hard, although for him relatively easy, but doing them one after another, and at that angle! For the average climber, just hanging on to those holds and at that angle would be an achievement – moving on them would be another matter.

The route stands out as a monument to the power and determination that has made Jerry Moffat one of the world's greatest rock climbers. Will this prove the high-water mark of his career?

Liquid Amber. Climber: Ben Moon.

—— 43 ——

GROOVED ARETE

Sitting at the haven looking at the view, I knew it had been the right move to leave the Peak District that morning.

Another jet whooshed past below us and the clouds continued to stream past above our heads. 'This beats working', I thought as I looked up at the overhang of Belle Vue Bastion.

The first few pitches had been easy but very polished, and we had put a rope on when it had started to get wet and polished. Ever since reading about the death of Jimmy Jewel I had been very cautious about soloing wet routes, no matter how easy. The lesson I had learnt was, it only takes one slip.

The holds streamed past, as did the Knights Move Slab, easier than expected, and the crux (I thought) was the groove on the third pitch. It was getting very cold now and we motored to the top to be enveloped in cloud, catching occasional glimpses of the valley below.

I was pleased we had done the route. I'd wanted to climb it since I first started climbing. Even now it was a great experience.

Tryfan.

The first section of the route.
Climber: Peter Menke.

The Knight's Move Slab.
Climber: Peter Menke.

—— 44 ——

TENNIS SHOE

The initial slab. Climber: Len Lovatt.

The setting is quite superb. Climber: Len Lovatt.

Noel Odell was the last man to see Mallory and Irving alive, on Everest in 1924. I saw him lecture about this in London, a frail old man who needed help to get to a taxi.

Back in 1912 he would have been young, spying the line of Tennis Shoe on the Idwal Slabs and climbing it solo, in the footwear that gave the route its name. Those were carefree days.

The Idwal Slabs are one of the most popular places for those starting to climb. The slabs are usually packed, the path up to them well worn.

Tennis Shoe is the best route here, taking a line up the left-hand side of the slab. The difficulties are moderate, if the protection is a little sparse, the route saving its hardest moves for the final tower.

Climb Tennis Shoe on a sunny day and you will be rewarded with great rock, great climbing and great views. The ghosts of those early Edwardian climbers will be there with you; how different it must have been back then!

—— 45 ——

DIRECT ROUTE

It means getting up early if you want to climb the Direct Route and enjoy it. There are two reasons for this. The first is the position of the crag, facing north on the south side of the pass; to get the sun an early morning start is necessary. The second is to avoid the crowds, especially on those busy bank holiday weekends when there are continuous streams of people marching up to the crag, and maybe twenty people on the Route at the same time.

The first pitch of Direct Route. Climber: Nick Mathews.

The famous hand traverse. Climber: Nick Mathews.

If you get it to yourself it is a far more pleasant experience as the route itself is really good: it takes a direct line up the centre of the nose of Dinas Mot. The first pitch follows slabs and then a groove to a stance before the famous hand traverse. The traverse itself looks daunting but turns out to be OK – there are foot holds, although small ones. The traverse leads to a huge ledge and the crux of the route. The move off the ledge into the final cracks proves hard – a foot on one wall, a stretch up for the crack, then keep the power on.

If you're not careful you will be racing with other parties to get up the route. Some people do not understand the ethics of climbing and will start climbing a pitch while you're leading it. Give them short shrift, but better still, get on it early.

The hard moves getting started on the top pitch. Climber: Nick Mathews.

—— 46 ——

LEFT WALL

Everyone has seen it and most people will have been inspired by it. Some will have been awestruck at the sight of Dinas Cromlech standing high on the hillside halfway down the Llanberis Pass. The fantastic sheer-walled buttress could have been architecturally designed, so perfect are its proportions and correctness of line.

Dinas Cromlech was at the forefront of climbing development in the fifties, sixties and seventies and remains a crag where everybody must climb. Following the breakthrough of Brown in the fifties (Cenotaph Corner), Livesey in the seventies (Right Wall) and Fawcett in 1979 (Lord of the Flies) it is now, according to Jerry Moffat, old-fashioned and easy.

The best route, however, is Left Wall. First climbed in 1956 with aid by R. Moseley, J. Smith

The Cromlech.

and J. Sutherland, the route wasn't freed until 1970. It is now a trade route with a continuous stream of climbers, much the same as Comes the Dervish. There is much debate as to the grade. It gets E2 although a lot of people say it is quite hard for that and may warrant E3. It is certainly a route to do if you are fit: nowhere is it that hard, but there is a lot of it, and the crux is the top crack, although there is a good rest before this. The line of the route is obvious and elegant. It takes a forked crack at the left-hand side of the left wall of the corner, hence its name.

The Cromlech is an intimidating place. It is difficult to get a level footing at the bottom of the crag; you are always craning your neck to look upwards at the towering faces and corners above. The rock is not the best, being a little shattered, and the gear can be suspect, although it's good on Left Wall. The Cromlech, however, is a place that has to be climbed on, even after the steep and knackering walk up.

I am told that Jimmy Jewel walked up, soloed Left Wall and walked down again, all within twenty minutes. Onlookers were impressed, more by the fact that he walked up and back so quickly than that he had soloed the route!

On the first part of the crack. Climber: Zoe Panchic.

Starting on the final traverse. Climber: Zoe Panchic.

—— 47 ——

CEMETERY GATES

One of Brown and Whillans' best and most famous routes, Cemetery Gates has stood the test of time and the passing of many hands and feet better than some of their other creations, including the more obvious Cenotaph Corner, which, although a good route, does not come into the same class.

Cemetery Gates follows a crack line on the right of the right wall of Dinas Cromlech. Starting on the left of the right arete the route swings left on to the right wall to enter the crack. The crack is followed to some fingery moves, which after some effort lead to a ledge. This isn't the belay, however, and more moves are made until another ledge is reached. This is the girdle ledge and the belay. The belay is in a magnificent position. Not only does the crag drop away below your feet but the ground drops steeply away below that, giving the most incredible sense of exposure. The first pitch would make a good route in itself. The belay adds to this, and the top pitch is the icing on the cake. Technically easier than the first pitch but with incredible exposure, the arete is followed on good positive holds, so look down and enjoy being right 'out there'. It doesn't last long enough before the forest is reached and you can lash yourself to the surprisingly large and sturdy trees. If you've got sandwiches this is a great place for a picnic! Take care when abseiling off, as the ropes can get stuck and it's a long boring walk around to climb back down and free them.

The route is no longer at the forefront of climbing and can be enjoyed by you or me. That's something I'm glad about.

Yarding up the top arete with a not inconsiderable amount of exposure. Climber: Martin Crook.

MAIN WALL

Cryn Las.

As you drive down the pass craning your neck to look at the Cromlech, take a look up the other side, up toward the Crib Goch ridge to the back of Cwm Glas. There you will see (if the cloud base is high enough) a fine cliff, Cryn Las. Get the sun at the right angle and the cliff will look down on you, a sinister skull, with its sunken eye sockets and broken nose. Then check the guidebook, and you will see three star routes at a range of grades, the oldest and best being Main Wall.

Do not be put off by the walk. It only takes about three-quarters of an hour and is pleasant in the extreme; if you take your time it will seem less of a chore, more of a pleasure in itself.

The bottom of the cliff is broken, so after a rest from the walk, gear up but don't rope up and scramble to the start of the climbing proper. First you go up a slab and then up what is probably the crux of the route, a rightward sloping ramp. This brings you to a triangular slab and peg belay. From this belay you swing out to the left and climb leftwards and upwards to the real pleasure of the climb, a slab; this is right on the edge of the cliff above Great Gully, and, with many holds and a great deal of exposure, leads to the top of the cliff and a descent down one or other side.

The route has a big feel about it, with not only climbing but route-finding difficulties. It's high up and a long way from the road. Essentially it has everything to be the perfect mountain route, except, perhaps, finishing on top of a mountain.

The top slab of Main Wall.

——— 49 ———

THE RAINBOW OF RECALCITRANCE

From the road that drops down into Llanberis from the pass, the Rainbow Slab can be seen, smooth yet rippled, its only features being a prow near the top and the rainbow itself, crossing the slab in a rainbow shape.

From the road the slab does not look very big, so vast are the quarries in which it is set. The sheer volume of rock that has been moved, by hand, is quite amazing. The scale of the place is emphasized once you are standing at the bottom of the slab. The slab is 150ft high and the routes look long and holdless. Once at close quarters more features are revealed, the crack lines of Pull My Daisy and Naked Before the Beast. The Rainbow of Recalcitrance starts up the latter and consists of thin crack climbing with equally thin protection. A step across on to the Rainbow itself leads to thin moves where the climber has to teeter along the rainbow. Good wires bring some relief before more teetering to a bolt, which is unfortunately hard to clip. Yet more teetering leads to a stance and a big sigh of relief. It is now the turn of the second. Seconding is no easier than leading as the swing potential is just as high. The second pitch, although easier, continues in the same vein and is even more poorly protected, until a small ledge and a peg are reached. Another sigh of relief is permitted at this point and a groove is then followed to the top. Again the second is not going to find things much easier so be ready for the swing. A fall is more painful to pride than body. As Chris Plant told me 'I fell off seconding the first pitch and firsting the second pitch.'

If you fall, run!
Climber: Ben Pritchard.

CENTRAL SADNESS

The Llanberis slate quarries have a special aura of their own, exuding a kind of mysticism, probably a relic of their industrial past. The spirits of long-dead miners haunt the holes and tunnels, the enormity of the quarries a testament to the years of back-breaking toil that created them. The last ladders and blast shelters are the only solid remnants of the quarries' human past.

The quarries can be a dangerous place. There are plenty of loose boulders, some razor sharp. The tunnels linking the holes are not as solid as they seem, the tunnel into the Lost World having recently collapsed.

It is through such a tunnel, leading from the far side of Dali's Hole – a surreal hole in the ground with semi-exposed trees and buildings, depending on how much water is in it at the time – that access to California is gained. Once inside, the walls tower above, giving a feeling of claustrophobia. The main wall looks smooth and the climbing improbable. The central line taken by Central Sadness is the longest and best.

The climb has two pitches, both E5 6a, the first poorly protected and the second well protected with a bolt belay in between. The climbing on the

Check the runout on the first pitch.
Climber: Steve Meyers.

first pitch is bold, the crux being the initial crack, while the second pitch is technical in an 'out there' position.

Central Sadness is a route of contrasts in a place that is at odds with the natural country from which it was created.

The second pitch is safer but more technical.
Climber: Steve Meyers.

—— 51 ——

THE DARK HALF

Climbing in the slate quarries of Llanberis has two dimensions. The big slabs with spaced protection typical of the first phase of slate development, and represented by such routes as Central Sadness, provide one dimension. The Dark Half represents the other face of slate climbing: steeper, bolt-protected, with super technical problems, where the holds and moves are not obvious. There are many fine routes in this category, all of which take a certain amount of lateral thought to work out. The Dark Half is the best. Created by slate guru Nick Harms, it is to be found up on the Manatese level opposite the Rainbow Slab. A line of bolts up a featureless wall of smooth black slate shows the location of the route. The climbing is very technical, a crutch-wrenching, shoulder-height rockover at halfway being the most improbable move.

The route is a test piece and it is unlikely to be climbed on sight. Just working out the moves will take some time and then linking them . . .

The Dark Half. Climber: Nick Harms.

—— 52 ——

COMES THE DERVISH

Looking out from Pete's Eats at the by now familiar Dervish slab with the white streak running up its middle – the line of Comes the Dervish – you can reflect that it was from just such a position that the inspiration for the route and the real start of the slate boom was born.

It was from here that Stevie Haston saw the line and, armed with the fork he had been using, abseiled the slab, cleaned out the crack and climbed the route, which at the time was E5 6a. The grade has been reduced as with the passage of many climbers (I know one Llanberis habitué who has climbed it more than ten times) the runner placements have improved. It is now said to be getting harder again as the holds are getting more rounded.

After finishing breakfast, take a stroll over to the quarries and the height and angle of the slab become apparent. It is a slab, but a steep one.

Gearing up on the sloping slate scree below the route, you can reflect again that the protection is bombproof and it's only 5c.

After 10–15ft of climbing, you are presented with a rockover, the first gear comes after the rockover and many climbers decide at this point that, well, maybe it can wait for another day. (When I climbed the route, three people who came along later decided to do exactly that.)

A confident attitude will reap benefits – the rockover isn't that hard, although somewhat polished – and from then on until above the overlap the protection is superb. The climbing is superb as well, sustained at a reasonable level, with the crux about 15ft below the overlap. From just below the crux you can look back down the line of Flashdance, to the position of the R.P. and contemplate how close to the ground you would be in a fall from here. The moves through the crux, which is where a lot of people fail but is not really any harder than the rest of the route, and on to the overlap take a bit of thought. Then you're cruising, but hold on, the holds are getting a bit flaky and the gear a bit sparse, so don't get carried away.

Comes the Dervish is such a fine route it deserves to be flashed. Anything else would be disappointing. The route is also very popular so don't try it until you can do it.

The climbing is superbly technical all the way.
Climber: Bob Wightman.

THE AXE

The Axe.
Climber: Dave Towse.

It's a solo now, isn't it?

OK, so an exceptional climber, the late Jimmy Jewel, soloed the Axe and was captured on video doing it. For mere mortals the thought of soloing such an 'out there' route is not one to be contemplated with a clear head, or to be voiced where anyone is likely to be within earshot.

The Axe takes the fine undercut arete high on the left side of the pinnacle which sits atop the east buttress of Clogwyn Du'r Arddu. The climb takes you through a roof low down, which is actually the crux of the route, before gaining the arete itself. The arete is what the climb is about, airy climbing in a position of sensational exposure.

Early morning is the best time to be here; as the crag is east-facing it catches the sun then. It is a quiet, solitary experience, a fine climb in a fine mountain setting.

—— 54 ——

OUTSIDE EDGE

Outside Edge is one of *the* classic mountain routes. It is high up in Cwm Silyn and was first climbed in 1931. It climbs a diagonal line up the great slab of Cwm Silyn and then follows the edge of the slab to the top of the crag. It is not as long as Grooved Arete, yet because of the gap in the middle of that route, has a not dissimilar feeling, size wise. The lake below glistens in the evening sun and the views are wide and far-reaching.

It is a route that any climber should climb, be they climbing at the grade (VD), when they will gain the greatest sense of achievement, or climbing much harder, when the situations will be enjoyed without any problems with the climbing.

There is also a sense of history about climbing at Cwm Silyn. It is not a modern crag, and high up on Outside Edge images of climbers from a distant age will come to mind – tweed-clad with big boots and hemp ropes, with no gear and not knowing what was coming next.

As you climb effortlessly in modern boots with modern protection, think back: the view will not have changed much, just the people.

Outside Edge. Climber: Mark Lyndon.

—— 55 ——

CRAIG DHU WALL

Some absolute classics can be very disappointing. They may have achieved their popularity from a particularly good photo, or because they were important at the time, or because they are accessible, or a host of reasons that do not necessarily relate to the quality of the climbing.

Others may actually be very good but have suffered from their popularity and are made unpleasant by the polished nature of the holds. Craig Dhu Wall is a very popular, very classic Severe that overcomes this problem by the brilliance of the climbing it offers.

Having actually located the crag and the school where you park, which isn't signposted, it may prove a little tricky finding the way to the bottom – which field should you cross and which field shouldn't you cross?

The route line is obvious from below – it follows the left-hand buttress of the crag. The route is described in the guidebook as having three pitches; with double ropes, it is quite practical and more usual to run the second and third pitches together. This makes the crux, which is quite high on the third pitch, more exciting, as one is out of touch and out of sight of the second.

The first pitch follows cracks into a V groove and then up to a very large belay ledge. From here a traverse out left presents one with the problem of whether to stand on the good holds and shuffle out, or sort of monkey along them with hands and legs hooked around. This feels more secure but looks horrendous and is a right old thrutch.

After going round the corner the climbing is just great, following good holds and good gear, but also requiring a certain amount of thought. High up now and out of sight of the second the crux is found. It really does take some working out: the move involves pulling up steeply on to a sloping and polished platform. It feels very precarious as it is quite balancy and strenuous all at once. A positive approach will bring a positive result. After this a breath can be taken and the rest of the climb completed without too much trouble.

Craig Dhu Wall.

The traverse on pitch two.

—— 56 ——

VECTOR

Tremadoc is that most popular of places, a road-side crag. There are several different crags that make up the area running along the road from Beddgelert to Tremadoc itself. On the southern edge of the Snowdon massif Tremadoc often attracts fair weather when the mountains are wet. It was because of these two advantages, ease of access and relatively good weather, that Tremadoc originally became popular. There are a lot of good routes here, too.

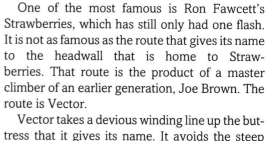

The traverse on pitch three.

One of the most famous is Ron Fawcett's Strawberries, which has still only had one flash. It is not as famous as the route that gives its name to the headwall that is home to Strawberries. That route is the product of a master climber of an earlier generation, Joe Brown. The route is Vector.

Vector takes a devious winding line up the buttress that it gives its name. It avoids the steep bulging lower walls and the steep smooth headwall by weaving a way between them. It originally had an awesome reputation for difficulty that has somewhat diminished today. It is a popular bank holiday outing for many, who underestimate its difficulties and are spurned low down.

The start is ignominious: not far from the road and amongst the trees, it does not inspire. Once the first 40 feet or so are out of the way the climb starts to show its mettle. There are hard moves getting to the obvious and now famous Ochre Slab. Once the slab has been gained the difficulties are not all over, delicate climbing leads up the slab, and then easier climbing to a cave where a belay is taken. A sense of relief will be felt, and not unfairly so. A traverse leads off to the left, the bulges of the lower wall below, the overhanging face of the headwall above. It's all easy now, except there is a sting in the tail – a steep and difficult little crack that leads quickly to the top and safety.

It's not far to get back to the road and a welcome cup of tea at Eric's Café, which is the third good reason to be climbing at Tremadoc.

Vector: the hard moves to get to the Ochre Slab.

SYMPHONY CRACK

Peering over the top of the crag, the sea raging below, Symphony Crack looks like it should be much harder than it is – a perfect, square-cut corner like a mini Cenotaph Corner above the sea only grades easier.

Symphony Crack is at Rhoscolyn, the big little crag at the south side of Holyhead. It is different in character to Gogarth yet it is similar too. The village of Rhoscolyn is quite posh. Holiday homes stretch inland from a beautiful beach and perfect harbour protected from the sea by jagged islands that bar its entrance.

The crag is so different, wild and exciting, so elemental and so vital. Symphony Crack is a short route but a route that delivers so much for its size. To get to it you must scramble to the end of the headland, then traverse back in above the sea until just below the corner. Then it's straight up, elegantly bridging with good holds and superb protection all the way. If the sea is rough this will be the most exciting Diff you'll ever climb.

Symphony Crack. Climber: Len Lovatt.

—— 58 ——

THE MOON

Gogarth can be split into two areas, the lovely white quartzy rock of the Upper Tier to North Stack and the other material that runs south from South Stack.

In this second area are Mousetrap Zawn, Red Walls, Castle Helen and the Yellow Walls. The latter are steep and contain some great climbs, including the Moon, a route which is quoted in the guidebook as 'only the best route in the world'.

Yellow Walls lie directly below Ellins Tower, a building on the edge of the cliff that is now an RSPB information centre. This in turn is below the South Stack Café, which should not be missed when visiting Gogarth. It has rather short opening hours, about 11 a.m. to 6 p.m., and the most amazing staff. Everyone who works there moves in slow motion. I have never known people to be so slow without actually stopping. I've watched them and they are doing something towards serving you all the time but it still takes about five minutes to get a cup of tea, even if you are first in the queue. Everything in the café, however, is delicious or scrumptious or refreshing – it's great.

Having had a cup of tea and cake and conse-

The upper pitch is exposed. Climber: Mike Turner.

quently enforced relaxation you will be absolutely raring to go. A short walk and long abseil to the right of Ellins Tower will bring you out on a spur at the left of the crag. From here the Yellow Walls are very impressive. They are steep and overhanging. The throat may at this point go a little dry, but don't worry, the beauty of the Moon is that it takes a line through all this at a surprisingly easy standard (E3). There are three pitches. The first is short and fairly easy and goes up a groove. The second pitch goes up rightwards to a peg, then traverses right across a slab in an incredible situation to a groove, which is then descended to a belay. From the belay one moves rightwards again, then up to a groove, which is followed to the top. In the right weather the views of the Llyn Peninsular are lovely. You can sit in the sun as your second struggles up, looking at the view while the tourists look at you.

The top of Yellow Walls with the Llyn Peninsula in the distance.

—— 59 ——

HUNGER

The main cliff at Gogarth is a place for the adventurous among us. It is a place where we can commit ourselves to running it out on steep rock, always on sight, even on new routes.

There are many fine routes here but Hunger is the best. It takes a central line up the main wall, first following a discontinuous crack, then making powerful moves left to an overhang. All of this is somewhat overhanging and uses often large but rounded holds. The protection is good, although any pegs encountered should be treated with care. Some have rotted away in their placements, the eyes of others have the thickness of a ringpull.

The moves left lead to a roof. Once this has been surmounted, the first pitch, but not the climb, is over.

The next two pitches get technically easier as height is gained. The situations are superb, the angle still steep and the climbing still interesting. Being high in the middle of the main cliff is a wonderful position, the cliff is just so big. There is no other way to go than up: at this point you are committed. That commitment will pay dividends: when you sit in the grass and flowers at the top, the feeling of satisfaction is great. It's unlikely you'll want to do another one that day, there is too much in Hunger to reflect upon.

The main cliff is big. Climbers: Alistair Hopkins and Paul Pritchard.

The steep lower wall of Hunger gives sustained pumpy climbing. Climber: Alistair Hopkins.

The second pitch.

—— 60 ——

DREAM OF WHITE HORSES

Dream of White Horses is one of the most famous and probably one of the very best routes in England and Wales. The name alone is inspirational, the first ascensionist an inspired if controversial climber.

A first sight of Wen Slab will leave you thinking, 'Wow, I've got to climb on that!' There are a number of routes that go straight up, the best traverses the whole slab.

Standing on the promontory opposite, the slab looks quite steep and in places quite holdless. Do not be put off, the grade takes the situation into account. The climb is covered in good holds and is easy angled all the way.

There are two possible starts, one at sea level

The last pitch proves the crux, traversing above Wen Zawn on dubious rock.

and one from halfway down the far side. The latter is less satisfactory, although easier to get on to, avoiding the necessity to abseil. For me it is important to start sea cliff routes near the sea, and the traverse start misses that commitment. The slab is traversed, with the prospect of the final pitch getting ever nearer. This last pitch traverses steeper, less stable-looking rock right above the cave of Wen Zawn.

It's your mate's lead, and as he traverses away it becomes obvious that it's not as hard as it looks. There are big holds and good gear in abundance. The situation is superb and should be enjoyed. The amount of gear used will make the route more or less exciting for the second. Back on top the satisfaction of completing the route will be great, even if you've found it easy. It's one of those routes that just has to be climbed.

—— 61 ——

BRITOMARTIS

*The main pitch of Britomartis is quite superb.
Climber: Kath Goodey.*

Wen Slab sports a number of brilliant routes, but by concentrating on these the majority of climbers will miss the hidden gem that is Britomartis. Have you ever thought, when standing on the promontory looking at Wen Slab, what might be below?

On the seaward face of the promontory, only visible from North Stack, is Britomartis.

Although the same grade as Dream of White Horses (HVS) it is a route in total contrast.

Having abseiled down the Trap you will find yourself on a platform. This is the belay. The route takes the wall around to the right and cannot therefore be seen until the initial descent and traverse has been made. This wall is probably vertical although it feels as though it is slightly overhanging. The route takes a line of large holds up the centre of the wall, but thankfully the holds are very big otherwise the route would certainly be grades harder. There is no real crux, just a lot of the same thing. It is important to stay cool, otherwise although the holds are big, the angle would produce pumped forearms by the time the semi-hanging belay is reached, just after the *in situ* seagull!

The belay is an exciting place to be, especially if this is the first time on a sea cliff, and affords an excellent view of the second as he climbs the wall below. The next pitch has one slightly awkward move to get on to a platform and then traverses to finish up a scrappy groove and arrive on top of the promontory facing Wen Slab and the crowds on Dream of White Horses.

Britomartis is a fine route, with a big feel and sense of isolation about it. To do this route and Dream of White Horses on the same day would provide an excellent and contrasting day's climbing.

Making a hard pull on one of the cruxes of Infidel.
Climber: Steve Gorton.

Second Generation. Climber: Jas Sharpe.

Above the crux of Lean Machine the angle doesn't ease and the boulders seem far below. Climbers:
Pete Oxley and Mike Eden.

Enjoying the exposure on the top groove of Polaris.

Cider Soak. The wall overhangs. Climbers: Ian Vincent and Dave Thomas. ➤

Passing the old peg on Conger, the sea looking inviting below. Climber: Dominic Cook.

Reaching the belay on Dream Liberator. Climber: Steve Anson.

◄ *Thin moves at the start of Sacré Coeur. Climber: Fiona Lloyd.*

The top arete of Last Dancer. Climber: Rowland Edwards.

Liquid Amber's first ascensionist Jerry Moffat.

◄*The rising traverse of Lucky Strike.*
Climbers: Zoe Panchic and Nigel Fawthrop.

The final tower on Tennis Shoe. Climber: Emilly Lloyd.

Teetering along the Rainbow of Recalcitrance.
Climber: Dave Towse.

◄ *High on the first pitch of Cemetery Gates.*
Climber: Martin Crook.

An outrageous rockover on the Dark Half.
Climber: Nick Harms.

Outside Edge. Climber: Emilly Lloyd.

The Hollow Man. Climber: Mike Turner. ➤

The top pitch of Britomartis is less technical but more satisfying. Climber: Kath Goodey.

Darius is technical and sustained. Fiona Lloyd is on the crux.

London Wall is the perfect crack climb. ➤
Climber: Tony Ryan.

The final moves on Beau Geste. Climber: Simon Nadin.

Pebble Mill. Climber: Robin Barker.

Cranking up Wellington Crack.
Climber: Fred Simpson.

The angle eases at the top of
Supercool but the holds are
small and sloping.
Climber: Martin Atkinson.

Obsession. ➤
Climber: Rachel Farmer.

High on the Groove. Climber: Chris Plant.

The start of Hell's Wall. Climber: Sean Myles.

—— 62 ——

THE HOLLOW MAN

This is the best route on North Stack, better and harder than the Cad. The Hollow Man takes a parallel line up the wall right of the Cad, crossing The Bells! by the peg. Everyone who has been to Gogarth will have seen North Stack from the promontory above Britomartis, or sticking out in the distance on the other side of the main cliff from where the descent is made down the Gun Barrel.

It is not so often that they will have seen people climbing on North Stack. There are easier routes, from E1 upwards, but it is the hard routes from E5 upwards that draw the attention, even though climbers who are willing to go on these routes are fairly few and far between.

North Stack.

Why? Because the climbing here is very bold. Some of the routes can be fallen off, but it is not to be recommended. It is not a place for working and redpointing but for on-sight climbing, coming to terms with your own fears, and exploring the possibilities of what your mind can convince your body to do, even though the same mind is saying 'no!' It is a place where a route can be savoured in reflection, the memories of which will stay for a long time – memories of the rock, of small things, bits of lichen, colours, temperature . . . Climbing will be carried out in silence; the climber will become so immersed in his immediate space, the next hold, the next move, that time stands still. You will not hear someone on the Hollow Man saying 'This is great fun I'm having!'; North Stack is where the art of climbing takes on a Zen aspect.

**PART 3
THE NORTH**

—— 63 ——

VALKYRIE

There are two Valkyries on Peak gritstone. Both are HVS and both have two contrasting pitches. Valkyrie at the Roaches is the superior one of the two. The two pitches are different in character and both interesting. The first pitch is a crack with bulges and looks as though it is going to be quite hard and strenuous but turns out to be fairly easy, if the trouble is taken to work it out. At the top of the crack a little traverse leads to a large flake and belay.

The view from here is great; you can see a long way above the trees and Rock Hall, now deserted, and this is a great place for contemplation. It may be worth considering the second pitch. This descends the far side of the flake before a long and very tricky step is made to better holds. This step is made out to the prow above a large overhang, increasing the feeling of exposure. Rounding the prow the difficulty eases and an easy slab is followed to the top of the crag and a belay, which may be awkward to arrange.

As with other routes at the Roaches, Valkyrie is a route of variety, with a feeling of quality often missing from other gritstone crags. It looks harder than it is but still requires thought. An excellent all-round route.

The Valkyrie buttress.

--- 64 ---

PEDESTAL CRACK

Being south-facing, the Roaches is often warm and dry when other crags are still wet. It is often a lot warmer than the eastern edges, for example, as it doesn't catch the wind in the same way but does catch the sun.

The central wall with its huge overhang, the home of Sloth, sports an unlikely and excellent VD. Pedestal Crack manages to avoid the overhang by traversing left on a parallel line of foot and hand holds, which seem to have been created to be climbed on. This leads to a corner with a tricky move to enter it. If done in one pitch, care should be taken to avoid unnecessary rope drag. After this the corner leads via large holds to the top.

If the route is climbed in two pitches, the second will belay on top of the Pedestal, the large flake in the middle of the wall from which the route derives its name. The top of the Pedestal can be reached up either side. From this belay the roof above can be fully appreciated, with the lines of Sloth and the even more outrageous Painted Rumour to wonder at.

Pedestal Crack.

—— 65 ——

SLOTH

'Compulsory three-toed sloth!' would be the order from the chairman on the coach on the Easter rugby tour. Everyone would hang upside-down from the luggage rack.

It is roughly the same position that is achieved when going through the roof of Sloth. If ever there was a feature that demanded to be climbed then this is it. The roof of Sloth is about 50ft above the

ground and juts out about 15ft. The climbing is not hard as there are massive flakes to hold on to and get your feet inside before the crux, which is achieving a standing position above the lip of the roof. It is just persuading yourself from so far below that this is the case.

It is the hand jams of Don Whillans that you are following, but whilst making the moves through the roof there will be no time for reflection, just do it!

The roof of Sloth. Climber: Nick Barraclough.

—— 66 ——

DARIUS

I wonder how many motorists have almost had accidents while craning their necks to get a better view of those crazy people moving ant-like high up on the appropriately named High Tor. How many holiday-makers have been surprised when walking along the top of the crag and someone appears over the top as if from nowhere. I also wonder how many arguments there have been between climbers and the landowners when they have been asked to pay to walk back down. Having had the skill and initiative to get up there without using the path you would have thought

High Tor: Darius takes a line up the centre.
Climber: Gareth Jones.

they would have been let off. In fact, I dare say that the landowners' profits have been boosted by tourists, attracted by the antics of the climbers.

Darius takes a central line up the highest part of High Tor. There are two pitches, the first a short E2 4c groove leading to a belay ledge. From here the big pitch begins and it really feels big. There are rests but the hard climbing continues all the way to the top. The route follows a flake and then moves right, up past a bolt – this is the crux – sidestepping back left on small holds. A final groove leads to the top and a hurried abseil back down before the landlords come looking for their money.

—— 67 ——

BODY MACHINE

Deep in the heart of the Peak District lies a tranquil river valley cut from the underlying limestone. It is peaceful and there is little traffic, except for the intermittent stream of cars heading to and from Raven Tor.

The fishermen continue to attempt to lure the trout into one false move while the climbers at Raven Tor 'work' their latest project.

Body Machine is one of the longer routes here. Climbed in one pitch it provides a stern test of technique, strength and stamina. The start is common with Indecent Exposure and the Prow. A monkey up a much abused and well-chalked tree is followed by the step on to the crag. Indecent heads left while Body Machine and The Prow follow a break rightwards. Body Machine breaks up a smooth white wall to a desperate rockover, which proves exciting if you are not tall enough to clip the bolt first. The climbing then becomes more sustained, until another hard move pulling on a small finger hold leads to the next break and a rest. From here the route steepens and becomes more powerful as moves are made through bulges. If you are anything other than fit, the route will find you out at this point as stamina is tested to its limit, before the lower-off and descent are reached.

*The hard rockover.
Climber: Felicity Butler.*

—— 68 ——

MECCA (THE MID-LIFE CRISIS)

Raven Tor is the home of hard sports-climbing in the UK.

At first acquaintance it does not look so impressive. It does not have the magnificence of Malham, but on closer inspection has an over-powering massiveness of its own. The steepness, the small holds, the powerful and sustained nature of the climbing all add up to make Raven Tor what it is today, a Mecca for hard climbers. On an average day at Raven Tor you could see any number of Britain's top climbers, hanging from bolts or reading the paper and just occa-sionally climbing. It's that sort of place – you don't actually spend that long on the rock, the routes are just too hard.

So what is special about Mecca? It is so sus-tained, with continual 6b moves with some 6c thrown in for good measure. Rests? Forget about them, there aren't any. The climb starts horizontally, then moves out from the bulging lower section on small holds to a hanging groove. The groove will sap all remaining stamina and it is only determination that will see the would-be

At the bottom of the groove. Climber: John Welford.

ascensionist get past it and to the lower-off. Countless times climbers have reached the top of the groove only to be rejected with success staring them in the eyes. But it draws climbers to it like pilgrims to Mecca, making it Britain's most popular 8b+.

Moving up the groove.

The climbing doesn't ease at the top.

--- 69 ---

MOONWALK

Moonwalk: the climber is making the hard starting move.
Climbers: Matt Saunders and Dave Turner.

Curbar has a reputation for hard routes. There are many here. Moonwalk is one of the great grit routes; it is not as well known as many others at Curbar, but for the grit connoisseur it is a masterpiece.

Short, sweet and very sharp. A desperate power move lifts you off the ground with an almighty heave, and it is touch and go whether you are actually going to get established on the route. Once above the initial moves, the climbing eases in the middle section, and then comes the crux. The gear is all right except there isn't much of it. A balance move on rounded slopes with the last protection below foot level makes it quite nervy. Make the move OK and it is not quite all over. More balancy, though easier, moves lead to the top and a sense of relief. Get it wrong and an unpleasant fall awaits.

Technical but safe moves lead out to the arete.
Climber: Peter Menke.

—— 70 ——

CHEQUERS BUTTRESS

The arete is nicely exposed. Climbers: Peter Menke and Sabina Gutte.

Froggatt Edge has many fine climbs. Walking along the bottom of the crag you go through a potted history of hard climbing in the past twenty years, from Great Slab through Hairless Heart to Beau Geste and Benign Lives, desperates in the modern gritstone idiom. It's the far end of the crag, though, where you will find Chequers Buttress, the finest route on the crag.

This piece of rock is just made to climb, luring you upwards via first an easy crack, then a bold swing out to the arete on superb, interesting natural holds. Airy moves are then made up the arete. The climb flows, and for full enjoyment so should you. The setting is great, the views are magnificent, and once you have completed the route The Chequers Inn will serve a refreshing pint. Highly recommended, oh, and so is the route.

— 71 —

BEAU GESTE

Moving around the arete of Beau Geste. Climber: Simon Nadin.

Beau Geste is an inspirational route. Much has been written about it but few have climbed it, even fewer on sight. Currently given E6 6c, the truth of the matter is that, like Strawberries, if you do it on sight (and, after all, it is supposed to be an on-sight grade), the route is E7.

First climbed by Johnny Woodward in 1982, in an inspired moment, it wasn't repeated for four years, which, in the Peak District, and for such a well-known route, is a long time.

Beau Geste is a great natural line, devious, technical, sustained and protected only just well enough to avoid all-out disaster.

The route follows a groove in the right of the arete to a break – so far so good – and protection with friends. It is at this point that the climber has to psyche himself up and stay cool. Difficult moves lead left around the arete, moving away

Pulling the pebble on the crux of Beau Geste. The result of failure – a ground-sweeping fall. Climber: Simon Nadin.

from the protection and towards an ever-more serious fall. Two belayers are necessary and at this point they will be tense and expectant. Crux moves using a small pebble enable you to gain a position from which a small wire can be placed in a crack on the left wall. Once clipped the ground-fall potential is past but the difficult climbing is not over. Hard moves up the arete lead to a better crack, at which point success is assured.

It must have been hard before Firés, it isn't easy with.

—— 72 ——

PEBBLE MILL

The crags of the Burbage valley are different in character and provide different climbing, though always of high quality. The residents of Sheffield are lucky to have these crags such a short drive from the city.

Burbage North is the most popular, with some superb middle-grade routes and some classic boulder problems. Burbage West is strictly bouldering country, West Side Story providing a test for any aficionado. Burbage South has hard grit routes of the highest quality, the best of the bunch being Pebble Mill.

On first sight, with no chalk to show the way, the initial slab of Pebble Mill looks blank. On closer inspection there is a way; it's technical, but once sussed, the opening moves are not too hard. The climbing has little to do with power and strength, more to do with balance and technique. The moves flow beautifully until standing on the slab, gripping the arete, all ready to barn-door off. It's just a case of staying in balance and stretching, but steadily, until the break is reached, giving a moment of relief. A quick pull around the corner and a ledge is reached – 'it must all be over now.'

The technicalities are, but if you're on the short side the scary bit is to come; if you are tall then it's just a case of reaching for the next break. Suddenly the route is over. Just like any good grit route Pebble Mill combines boldness with technicality and a most beautiful surrounding.

Moving up the 6b slab. Climber: Robin Barker.

Scary final moves. Climber: Robin Barker.

— 73 —

MUTINY CRACK

The sun is shining, the sky is blue, the rock is warm and everything is right with the world. The feeling of climbing on real rock in real sunshine after the winter's hibernation is hard to beat.

For many residents of Sheffield, Burbage North is the first piece of rock they will venture on to, eyes blinking, unaccustomed to the light after many evenings training in their cellars.

Bouldering, soloing, up and down, up and down, enjoying the feeling of freedom that comes when unhindered by ropes or the other para-phernalia of rock climbing. A great feeling of being alive that may lead to the odd route.

Mutiny Crack is, and yet isn't, an obvious feature. When walking along the path at the bottom of the crag it could be missed, yet once in close proximity the route is startlingly obvious. The crux is at the bottom. A pull and rockover through a roof, followed by a balance move lead to a series of overlaps on big holds; swinging up these is sensational. They lead to a holly bush and the top, where you feel the wind and get down quick for another route or to do it again. It is short but sweet – what gritstone is all about.

Mutiny Crack packs a lot into such a short route. Climbers: Hilary Gott and Dave Turner.

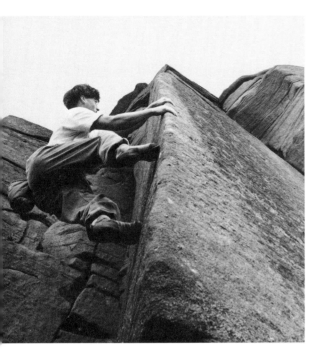

Archangel involves one technique: layback and smear. Climber: Matt Saunders.

ARCHANGEL

Stanage is the most traditional of crags, the most popular, the most overcrowded.

On a summer evening the parked cars stretch out along the road and the climbers stretch out along the crag. Of course there is always something to do, the classics are always busy, their polished nature a testament to their popularity.

The best route at Stanage and one that isn't likely to get too polished is Archangel.

Archangel is the obvious holdless arete left of Goliath's Groove, situated halfway along the crag above the Plantation Boulders. Before embarking on an ascent of Archangel it may be worth trying Crescent Arete, a similar problem on one of the boulders below. If this proves do-able then Archangel should be OK – it's just longer, higher and consequently more scary.

There is only one technique for climbing Archangel and that is to layback. The arete feels rounded but there are ripples that will provide more purchase. Stay cool and move quickly. there is no gear until the hard climbing is over, so don't worry about it. The buzz of the route comes from committing oneself with no gear and moving, and keeping moving.

Topping out. Climber: Matt Saunders.

— 75 —

EDGE LANE

When the quarrymen finished with Millstone they had done a pretty good job. The cracks were a bit thin, but with the help of aid, climbs were made usable. The aretes needed no further work.

Edge Lane, man-made though it is, is a fantastic feature: a perfect, soaring arete with just enough holds and no protection.

The climbing on Edge Lane is balancy and technical, with the hardest move at about three-quarter height. On-sighting the route would be hard as it is a solo, so most top-rope it first before committing themselves. It still feels hard and the adrenaline will be pumping on the crux.

Everyone wants to climb Edge Lane, everyone should climb Edge Lane, though for most people once is quite enough!

Edge Lane is the perfect arete, scary but superb.
Climber: Simon Creswell.

--- 76 ---

LONDON WALL

Do you remember the *Rock Athlete* series? I remember several parts – Ron Fawcett on Lord of the Flies, Jerry Moffat bouldering. The part I remember best was the film of London Wall. The climb seemed straight-forward enough, and the climber had his fingers in the crack, smeared with the feet – then his foot slipped and he was off.

London Wall is the perfect crack climb. It is a marvellous line, a finger-width crack splitting an otherwise blank wall. The crux is low down and once past this, success should be ensured. It isn't. The route is sustained and although there are no moves as hard, there are a lot of hard moves. It is longer and more sustained than most grit routes, so fitness is needed, not just bouldering power.

London Wall is such a good route it should be flashed, so save it until you are really fit.

Although the top is easier, it is where most climbers blow it. Climber: Tony Ryan.

—— 77 ——

THE RASP

Gritstone routes are usually technical and usually quite powerful; few are overhanging and pumpy, but the Rasp at Higgar Tor is such a route.

Higgar Tor is a leaning gritstone block that appears to have been prised away from the hillside to end up at its current tilted angle. The rock here is the roughest gritstone, seemingly designed specifically to abrade ropes and tear clothes.

The front face of the incredible leaning Higgar Tor provides steep pumpy climbing. Climber: Felicity Butler.

The Rasp looks straightforward enough, a line of large flakes leading up the centre of the leaning wall, followed by a traverse off to the right. The first moves are a bit slippery, but once the flake has been reached the climbing is easy enough, if steep. It is after a mass of *in situ* tat that the climbing gets hard. Having been laybacking up a large positive flake with plenty of footholds, the footholds suddenly disappear and the flake becomes rounded. It is here the angle really tells and the point at which the weak will be spurned.

The flake is nicely rounded.
Climber: Felicity Butler.

Get up this section and a delightful prospect is in store: a horrible traverse, or a desperate direct finish on totally rounded holds. The choice is yours, the Rasp will win either way.

The chin-grinding traverse.
Climber: Felicity Butler.

—— 78 ——

SIRPLUM

Since bolt-protection became commonplace on hard routes, Cheedale has become more and more popular. There are still plenty of non-bolt routes and these have grown in popularity as more climbers train on climbing walls that are modelled on limestone, so the real limestone routes consequently feel easier. There are a lot of very good routes down Cheedale but few exceptional ones.

One exception is Sirplum. Traditional and popular, Sirplum is a truly excellent route with few peers, not only in the Peak District but anywhere. I have not yet heard anyone disagree with this point of view. On the contrary, most people rave about the climb.

Why is it so good? Well, one look at Plum Buttress will tell you – a route that's HVS going through ground this steep! It does, but in a kind of sneaky, sideways way. Before the main pitch there is a preamble, a nice little warm-up pitch that leads, not as easily as first appearance might suggest, to a large ledge. From here the buttress sticks out and hangs overhead. There is a way through, heading out into the void and gradually upwards on large holds, weaving through roofs, feeling the exposure. The gear is good, there are *in situ* slings and a huge thread, but if you're not feeling confident don't look down. Soon the struggle is over and you're up. Now for the second. Did you place the gear close enough together in case he falls off? If he does, can he climb a rope to get back on?

It's a nice spot, there are wild flowers and blue skies and a tea van conveniently situated back where you parked. The climbing experience that is Sirplum should be enough for one day.

Plum Buttress is quite outrageously steep.
Climbers: Ian Smith and Nick Hepburn.

Sirplum takes an incredible line for its grade.
Climbers: Nick Hepburn and Ian Smith.

—— 79 ——

HIGH NOON

High Noon is as desperate as it looks.
Climber: Dave Hauton.

Caley is just outside Leeds. The crag cannot be mistaken as you speed out of town towards the Yorkshire Dales — there are loads of boulders by the side of the road to mark it. It is bouldering that Caley is best known for. If any climber were to discover Caley today they would be in raptures, the possibilities endless. It was, however, discovered a long time ago and the possibilities have been well tried.

Behind the boulder field there is a crag, which is rather nice, if little. A walk along the crag will reveal one outstanding feature, the soaring arete of High Noon.

High Noon is the time of all good gunfights. It is not the time to climb the route although the consequences could be equally painful. A slab on the left leads to some gear in a crack. That's it. After that it's caution to the wind unless you have sensibly top-roped first. Getting established on the arete is not easy. Getting up it is harder. It is a route that requires good friction, which means climbing it in autumn. If you are going to fall off then do it feet first on to the slab; at least that way you should avoid serious injury.

So you've done it, what's next? Well, there is another little arete over at Ilkley.

—— 80 ——

GREAT WESTERN

Almscliff is the most traditional of outcrops, a wart sticking out of the rolling fields west of Leeds. A carbuncle on the Yorkshire countryside, the crag that has a reputation for hard grades.

When you first get there after all the hype the crag is disappointing. It's quite small and, well, uninspiring. Until you get on to Great Western that is, which certainly packs it into its short length. Steep all the way, the route climbs first a corner crack, which is pumpy, then traverses under a roof. The traverse isn't easy, neither is placing gear. Needless to say the crux of the route comes at the end of the traverse. A long stretch is then needed to reach jugs. The tired climber, and many will be tired by this point, may find this all a bit too much and slump on to the gear. The go-for-it type will be rewarded by grasping a huge lump of nice rough Yorkshire gritstone.

This a place for the poseur, in front of the summer Sunday crowds mingling around the top and the bottom of the crag, cameras poised to get that vital snap of your fall from grace, and young boys and girls fascinated by the beauty of movement!

One more move to reach the jugs.
Climber: Fiona Lloyd.

--- 81 ---

WELLINGTON CRACK

Wellington Crack. Climber: Fred Simpson.

Wellington Crack is a sort of shorter, easier London Wall. It is just as good. Ilkley is a sort of smaller, less good, more windswept Millstone.

The crag overlooks Ilkley in the valley below and the countryside beyond. The town is not a climber's place. It seems somehow out of place, but the inhabitants like it.

The crag on the other hand, *is* a place for climbers. Tourists do come up here to admire the rather disappointing view, but climbers come here to do the business on the grit.

Wellington Crack is immortalized through the pictures in Dave Jones' *Power of Climbing*. John Dunne soloing in his Ninjas on an unfriendly looking day. For mere mortals a rack is recommended. There are plenty of places to slip in the wires.

The route follows a peg-scarred diagonal crack up an otherwise blank piece of slightly off-vertical grit. There is an edge at first for the feet but this runs out and the climber must keep the power on to the top. There are no rests.

—— 82 ——

THE ASHES

Kilnsey as a crag cannot be ignored: it has presence, its mighty bulk sitting there by the side of the road like a huge breaking wave frozen for all time.

Most famous for its main overhang, which isn't that big when compared with other roof routes the crag has, it has taken on a new popularity since the advent of sports-climbing. The potential of those huge leaning walls for pumping out not just forearms but the entire body, can be realized with nice lines of bolts.

The Ashes gives fine climbing in the modern idiom: hard, steep and safe. It is one of many lines that sit in the shadow of the main overhang. As such it stays dry most of the time. The start through the undercut at the bottom is all right and leads to exceptionally pleasant climbing, bridging up a wide groove. The standard so far has been about E3/4, 5c/6a, and very nice too. About two-thirds of the way up this all changes. The angle suddenly steepens, the quality of the holds deteriorates and you are launched into an exasperating sequence of 6b moves that test both mind and body alike. It is hard to hold on here, and to hold on and work out the moves is even harder. After some pretty wild moves a lower-off chain is thankfully reached.

Then it's back down to the ground to end up some way from the base of the crag, and this isn't even one of the steep routes.

Kilnsey. Matt Saunders climbing the Ashes.

The crux 6b sequence of the Ashes. Climber: Matt Saunders.

—— 83 ——

SUPERCOOL

Gordale: Supercool takes the steep wall left of the cracks.
Climber: Martin Atkinson.

The fantastic formations of limestone in Yorkshire are awe-inspiring sites for the public to visit. The sight of climbers inching up and then falling off these steep walls provides the icing on the cake.

Gordale is the least popular and also the least hospitable of the main crags. The routes here are big undertakings, the easier routes suffering from loose rock, the hard routes being long and the classic cave routes not yet bolted. If, or rather when, they are, their popularity will be assured. They are both big lines.

To the left of the cave routes is a steep smooth wall. This is taken head-on by Supercool, a more modern route. This is not a natural line, but a natural blank space; a line of, in places well-spaced, bolts shows the line of the route – that's if you can see all the bolts from the ground, which is not always easy.

Supercool has a number of problems with which the climber must deal. Complicated technical moves on mainly small and sloping holds are compounded by the length of the route. Added to this is the potential for a big fall. The reason for the name of the route soon becomes obvious.

Learning the moves, being fit enough and then keeping it all together is the name of the game on Supercool.

Not a hugely popular route, but an outstanding one. Just go and look at it.

—— 84 ——

OBSESSION

On the upper tier at Malham the atmosphere is different from the Catwalk. It is not the place to hang out but the place to go when you want to do a route, before returning to the Catwalk to inform the crowds of success or failure.

Obsession is the route that was the start of things to come at Malham. Bolt-protected, long and steep, it was a new style. The holds are good and the technical difficulty relatively low. What is needed is stamina, and a head for heights. It is airy up here, a long way down to the stream and the tourists in the valley below. Falling off gives a sensation of falling into the void, quickly stopped by a friendly bolt. The ground, though, is a worryingly long way off.

A route that will make a big impression on your mind, a route that you will rave about for a long time.

Obsession.

The Groove is one of the more obvious lines at Malham.
Climber: Chris Plant.

— 85 —

THE GROOVE

Malham is an absolutely outstanding crag in every way. It is the most magnificent piece of rock architecture. It is big, yet it has easily defined sections. It is a popular tourist attraction, and understandably so. The river flowing out from under the crag, and its rise or drop in level between the morning and evening, is a source of constant amazement.

There is one huge outstanding feature of the crag – a groove that runs straight up the centre. It is immensely long and steep, but was eventually climbed in its entirety in one pitch by John Dunne. This was a marvellous achievement that necessitated standing on a ledge halfway up while the second ran around to carry on holding the ropes. This was the idea – straight up the middle in one push, the ultimate pump pitch.

Soon the route had run into controversy. Glued-on holds were found on the top overhang, and no one knew who stuck them there. The route was devalued. Now it is the first half of the route that is climbed. It is still long enough and is a fine pitch in its own right.

A lot of effort is needed to get the redpoint. It just keeps on coming. It is not too hard technically, if E7 6b isn't hard, but it is sustained. There is the most peculiar hands-off rest, half-way up, where you stop with one leg hooked over a flake.

The line is superb, the route just has to be climbed.

Hard moves low down lead into the Groove itself.
Climber: Chris Plant.

—— 86 ——

ZOOLOOK

The superb natural amphitheatre that is Malham.

Zoolook. Climber: Perry Hawkins.

Shorter but more technical than the Groove, Zoolook is probably the most popular E7 at Malham.

It isn't that short either, especially when compared to the other routes in the area that are maybe half its length.

The crux comes low down, requiring outrageous moves to gain an obvious flake, and then to leave it. It is not all over here, though. The route carries on in a technical and powerful vein, most climbers losing it at about three-quarters height at an overlap. Back to the ground again. Rest, relax, then back on to try and solve that elusive sequence, such is the style of ascent of modern bolt routes. Keep trying this over several days and then it's time for the redpoint.

So some of you may be asking, what does 'redpoint' mean? Well, it is simply climbing the route from the ground to the top without falling off or resting on the rope or gear. Simple, isn't it?

—— 87 ——

OVERHANGING BASTION

The Castle Rock of Triermain.

The Castle Rock of Triermain. A name that brings romantic and dark images to mind. The crag has two aspects, one west-facing and slabby, the other north-facing and steep. It is the main feature of the north face, an overhanging ramp line, that is Overhanging Bastion, the route.

Popular because it is so good, the route is easy to locate. Once on the climb, the reason for its popularity soon becomes evident. The line is natural, the rock good and the climbing interesting. The gangway peters out near the top of the crag and it is here that the route packs its punch. The crag is steep. Wildly exposed, less well-protected moves on thankfully good holds lead up a wall. There is nothing between the climber and the ground below and the exposure is terrific, when a final slab and wall lead easily to the top, the adrenalin flowing.

The climb is over but the excitement remains. You'll be talking about that one for a while.

—— 88 ——

HELL'S WALL

For many, a visit to Borrowdale means one thing: bouldering at the Bowderstone. This giant boulder, with its steeply overhanging sides and nicely rounded, polished holds provides training *par excellence* for the already fit climber. So why else come here? Well, apart from the delights of Reecastle, Shepherds', Black Crag and so on, there is one very hard, very good route. It is on a little crag not far above the Bowderstone, from which the crag gets its name. The route is Hell's Wall.

To reach the route a bushwhacking walk straight up through the woods from the Bowderstone is undertaken. The trees here are so old. The rocks are so old, one might have been transported to a prehistoric site. The line of pegs running up the crack that forms the line of Hell's Wall brings you back to the present day and the job in hand.

There are so many pegs on Hell's Wall, a hangover from its days as an aid route, that it is difficult to clip them all. The pegs do enable you to approach the route as a sports-climb, failure on the first attempt leading to the redpoint. Even with all these pegs the start is a little bold. If you have any chance of making the crux moves then it shouldn't prove a problem, but be careful not to slip. The route is technical, the E6 6c crux being preceded and followed by sustained 6a/b climbing. There is, though, a very definite crux about a third of the way up. Fingers locked in the crack, the legs are raised high, pushing away on sideways edges. A long reach right for a better hold but . . . no, the foot has slipped again and you're resting on the peg, frustration starting to mount. A little, long-legged, small-bodied spider scuttles past, mocking the pathetic human attempts to emulate its ease of motion.

Successful or not you can relax in the most

The climbing is sustained at a high standard. Climber: Sean Myles.

wonderful of cafés down in Borrowdale. Take in the summer sunshine, have a cup of tea, eat some cake and let the beautiful world of the Lake District just flow by before – well, how about an evening at Reecastle?

—— 89 ——

TROUTDALE PINNACLE

Borrowdale in the centre of the Lake District is a valley frequented by Scout camps, walkers, tourists and climbers. It is home to the famous Bowderstone and many famous crags, and is a great base for a weekend's climbing.

Black Crag is set back from the road, halfway up the hillside, but is worth the walk to climb Troutdale Pinnacle. Standing on the Pinnacle itself is an exciting experience.

The climbing ambles its way up the crag via a short wall and slabby groove. All of a sudden you're a long way up and the views are getting

majestic. A traverse follows, towards the pinnacle. Then comes a short wall and you're standing on top of the pinnacle itself. From here the whole vista of Derwent Water, Keswick, Skiddaw and Blaencathra stretch out before you. It is a great place to drink in the special beauty of the Lake District. The best time to be there is late on a spring evening, the valley below thrown into shadow while you bathe in the last rays of the sun.

A short pitch follows to the top and then a walk back down a very loose scree slope.

The climbing experience is transitory, but the memory remains.

Black Crag, Borrowdale.

The easy angled lower pitches.

On top of the pinnacle.
Climber: Glen Rowley.

---- 90 ----

WHITE NOISE

Reecastle is billed as a perfect evening crag. This is because the sun setting in the west bathes Reecastle in a lovely warm light; the rock changes its colour and the whole character of the crag is altered. The routes that on a cold, windy day seem very hard, seem somewhat easier. They aren't, of course. There is something at Reecastle for everyone climbing HVS upward. There are classic hard routes such as Torture Board, and superb, though easier, climbs such as Guillotine. The best is White Noise.

The crag, which looks small from a distance, is bigger once you are standing underneath. It is barrel-shaped and so the top disappears after steep starts to the routes. Such is the case with White Noise. The route takes a thin crack line to the left of the central crack (the line of the Rack Direct, which is obvious even from the road). To get into the crack some steep moves on large holds lead to a sloper; there isn't any gear here, so a committing move has to be made to get into the crack. A friend in an obvious slot will slow the heartbeat, and interesting safer and easier angled climbing leads you up the crack line to the top of the crag. The route isn't just a one-move wonder although it does have a distinct crux. It is the perfect way to round off a day.

The difficult starting moves of White Noise.
Climber: Sean Myles.

White Noise.
Climber: Chris Plant.

PRAYING MANTIS

Traversing out of the chimney on pitch one. Climber: Chris Whitehead.

From Grange, Goat Crag is an ugly lump on the hillside. From the campsites by the river it is still fairly ugly, but is starting to look more interesting. After trailing up the screes, the crag can be fully appreciated, though it is not that inspiring, especially with the disgusting stench of the putrefying flesh of the dead sheep that litter the bottom of the crag wafting up into your nostrils.

Goat Crag, Borrowdale. Home of one of the routes with which Pete Livesey changed the climbing world in 1975. Footless Crow is not the best route here: that honour goes to an altogether more traditional and somewhat easier route, Praying Mantis. The northern aspect of Goat Crag was first revealed from layers of earth, moss and other undergrowth in 1965 when Praying Mantis was first climbed. No one bit of the route is outstanding in itself but it is the whole once brought together that provides a fine experience. The first pitch feels enclosed, climbing a crack-cum-chimney. The crux of the route is halfway up this pitch, where pumpy layback moves leave weaker climbers hanging from their gear, wishing they had warmed up better. A go-for-it attitude will reap dividends as it is only a few moves before better holds arrive. The second and third pitches weave their way first left and then right, delicate traversing on small holds back towards the overhanging part of the crag, which the route has so far sensibly avoided. The exposure increases but the technical difficulty is not great. Before the overhanging ground is reached the route heads back upwards, a wall and slab leading to the top. This is a classic route and also a good route, a route where the sum is greater than the individual constituent parts.

The hard move in the chimney on the first pitch of Praying Mantis. Climber: Chris Whitehead.

—— 92 ——

TOPHET WALL

Tophet Wall.

Mountains create their own weather. Masses of clouds can cover mountain summits while only a few miles away the valleys are basking in sun, or the tops of the mountains poke through into the sun while it is raining in the valleys. Such are the contrasts. Arriving in Wasdale on an afternoon of torrential rain, when the stacks of nearby Sellafield are stuck in the clouds, it is difficult to imagine that there are any mountains. If there are, they cannot be seen. Waking up the next morning to glorious sunshine the mountains are revealed and the eerie nature of Wastwater, the screes dropping straight into the water, is lessened.

It is mornings like this that make the bad days seem worthwhile. So how about going climbing? The crags hereabouts do not dry out instantaneously but climbing is possible. A nice long walk will get those muscles warmed up, so it's off to Napes Crag and an assault on Tophet Wall. From the valley it is difficult to imagine where the route goes, as the crag seems featureless, even the famous Napes Needle is indistinguishable from the mass. The walk up via Kern Knots takes time, but then Napes Crag is approached from the direction of Tophet Wall. Tophet Wall is tucked around the corner up a gully, with its famous and off-puttingly steep neighbour, Incantations. The gully is loose so care is needed when dumping rucksacks lest they slide off down the slope, depositing their contents in their wake.

Tophet Wall can be climbed in three pitches. The first takes you up an imperfectly protected wall and traverse to a good belay. By this point it will become apparent that the shaded nature of this side of the crag means that it is less than warm. With a wind howling down the gully, it is positively freezing. An exit can be made here for those with frozen fingers and toes; for the hardier

*The first pitch traverse.
Climber: Jane Stannard.*

the next two pitches provide the meat of the climb, varied climbing leading with ever increasing exposure upwards and rightwards to a pinnacle. The pinnacle is climbed, then a step back on to the wall allows a steep crack to be jammed until a ledge and easy climbing lead to the top.

The weather may be changing again now, the clouds coming back down the gully, the temperature dropping. A quick walk along the climbers' traverse and back down the spur to Wasdale and a well-deserved drink in the Wasdale Head Hotel are in order. This is a chance to reflect and decide what to climb next.

The view back down Wasdale from the climber's traverse.

--- 93 ---

BOTTERILL'S SLAB

It's a long walk but it's worth it. To climb such a feature in such a wonderful setting is well worth the hour and a quarter walk to get to it. I thought it would take longer but in the end it felt less of a drag than walking up to Dow Crag, which is lower but further in distance.

Everything about Wasdale and Scafell is magnificent, except, that is, for the motorway of a path that leads up to the saddle between Scafell and Scafell Pike. Like many of the paths in the Lake District it can be seen for miles – an ugly gash of brown against the green of the hillside. It is the worst kind of road, uncontrolled, sprawling, erosive. When walking up it, it appears in places to be as wide as a two-lane road. A two-lane road might actually be better as it wouldn't stand out as much and would save more of the hillside from being eroded. The National Park authorities should do more about footpath erosion, as should the BMC, rather than wasting their time worrying about bolting. I defy anyone to see a bolt until they are right under the crag, and even then it is not always easy, whereas these footpaths can be seen for miles. The authorities cannot do anything about bolting without licensing drills but they can do something about footpath erosion.

And so to Botterill's Slab. It is an obvious feature, slanting up the crag, and looks steeper from below than it actually is. As you get closer the expanse of Central Wall comes into sight and so does the line of Central Buttress, now horrendously polished. Botterill's Slab, which is in three pitches, was an outstanding ascent in its day, a step into the unknown. It is the middle pitch that is the essence of the route, being thin-slab climbing, taking the left-hand side, delicately and in a fine position. The views are equally fine, of Pike Crag and beyond.

After finishing the route, if it is hot, the stream on the walk down provides plenty of pools for swimming, and chutes to slide down – a very invigorating and refreshing end to a day in the hills.

Botterill's Slab, pitch one.

Botterill's Slab, pitch two.

—— 94 ——

BORDERLINE

Borderline: Ian Cummings on the second ascent.

You need to make an early start if you are serious about climbing on Scafell East. The crag high up on the east side of the summit of Scafell attracts only the morning sun and the morning climber. Although the crag's size is lost in the scale of the mountain, it is big enough to give a multiplicity of fine hard-rock climbs. It is unpopular enough still to have obvious unclimbed lines.

One of the more recent of these to be climbed was Borderline, the obvious steep overhanging groove and crack to the right of Ichabod. At E6 6c and that far up it does not see many repeats, but by all the accounts of those that have done it, it is a stupendous route. The first pitch tackles the groove and crack head on and took the first ascensionists some time to work out. The second pitch was climbed on sight at 6b. In all they were on the route for twelve hours! Do you fancy this after an hour and a half walk up?

—— 95 ——

ROARING SILENCE

On the East Buttress of Scafell there is a clutch of superb middle E-grade routes to go at. One of the lesser-known routes that will prove a wonderful find is Roaring Silence. The route takes a groove line breaking right out of Ichabod, which traverses in a horribly exposed manner above the over-hanging wall of Border-line. Such exposure is exhilarating in itself, but couple this to superb climbing and the spectac-ular mountain scenery round about and you have a fantastic pitch. It is not just one pitch, though, there are two. The second pitch does not let the first down, continuing the groove upward through the overhang to the right of the point crossed by Borderline. The two pitches are both 5c and are both worthy in their own right. It just leaves you asking the question, 'Why wasn't it climbed until 1979?'

The top pitch of Roaring Silence.
Climbers: Mark and Mike Hetherington.

— 96 —

ELIMINATE A

On a bank holiday weekend in the Lakes you can climb on Dow Crag to the sound of children swimming in Goat Tarn, youth groups shouting and screaming on the well-worn path up to the Old Man of Coniston and the chatter of the other hundred climbers on the crag.

On a weekday in the spring or autumn there is peace and quiet. The crag takes on an altogether bigger and more remote atmosphere and the climbs are better for it.

Eliminate A takes a weaving line up the left hand of the three buttresses. Traditionally, the route is climbed in seven pitches, but it is better to combine at least the first two, as these are short and pretty much in a straight line. Next comes a traversing pitch, which is more tricky, then the Rocher Perches pitch. This pitch is named after a number of perched blocks that, inevitably after all these years, are no longer there. The Rocher Perches pitch traverses under a large roof to a belay up on the left and has a definite feeling of exposure. The climb is very varied with the next pitches involving a chimney and a traverse across a slab, while the final pitch is a crack which leads to the top of the crag, from where you will still be able to hear the screams and shouts of the multitude, or, if you've picked the right day, the wind and the sheep.

The first pitch.

The Rocher Perches pitch.

The Rocher Perches pitch.

—— 97 ——

C ORDINARY ROUTE

The walk up to Dow Crag is pleasant. The crag is in view most of the time as the path gradually unfolds until Goat Tarn is reached. Dow looms above with the blue of the stretcher box standing out against the dark colours of the crag, sometimes grey, sometimes brown. From here the four buttresses A, B, C and D can be made out. C

The weather and setting are part of the experience.

Ordinary Route takes a direct line up the centre of C Buttress, 360ft of interesting and varied climbing unmarred by grassy scrambles between pitches. The direct line of the route and the consistency of the climbing make this an excellent route for a solo or for a beginner. The situation and views are wonderful. Even in bad weather, which is always quite likely in the Lakes, the route would be enjoyable. So enjoy the walk up, enjoy the walk down, but above all enjoy the climb.

—— 98 ——

TIGERS WALL

Northumberland is well known for hard boulder problems, but maybe less well known for outstanding routes. There are a number of these, and Tigers Wall matches up to any comparable climb anywhere. The setting is pleasant and remote, and the skyscapes can be quite stunning – the sky seeming bigger and more open here than in many other parts of the country. The views of the Cheviots are open and magnificent. The rock, which is a hard sandstone, has good friction and lacks the rounded sandy breaks of the sandstone in Kent. It is also possible to protect climbs here, though on many of the routes this protection is sparse.

Tigers Wall starts up a wall on small edges until an overlap is reached. A committing move through the overlap is then made to reach a flake that leads to the top. The climbing feels quite technical and the move through the overlap may make you think. The flake above is fun.

After climbing at Bowden Doors, an evening in Wooler should be enjoyed. Saturday nights are quite lively, a visit to the local disco being strongly recommended. Just tell them you know Watty.

Tigers Wall.

— 99 —

POSEIDON ADVENTURE

Poseidon Adventure is not a route for the faint-hearted. The gear is very sparse and where it does occur, which is in only one place, the break, it is not really very good. So get out your soloing head.

The Poseidon Adventure takes a line through the Wave. The Wave itself is a peculiar feature, a striated roof of rock running for a hundred yards or so above a slabby wall. The initial moves are technical and balancy E4 5c. Once a reach has been made for a small pocket the crux is a 6a pull on a small cusp and a long reach for the break. It

Poseidon Adventure. Climber: Steve Anson.

Catching the wave. Climber: Steve Anson.

would be possible to jump off from here without doing yourself serious injury. The next part involves jamming in an undercut and reaching through for the top of the crag. If you look up you can see straight through the wave to the jug at the top. Having got the top hold it's all over.

The climbing is nicely varied and sustained at its grade and has a distinct crux. The setting is quite wild for such a small and easily accessible crag. There are no trees and the Cheviots are visible in the distance. The sea can be seen from the top of the crag, but this is the most inland of waves!

—— 100 ——

RUSSETT GROOVE

Russett Groove. Climbers: Kath Gill and Jane Stannard.

It is seldom that one can find a Diff that brings a smile to the faces of those climbing about ten grades harder; Russett Groove is that climb. It is a delightful little route

Climbing can be fun. Climber: Kath Gill.

that will bring a smile to anyone's face, whether enjoyed roped or solo.

The climb takes small pockets on either side of a Glossgroove up towards a roof, which it then sensibly avoids on much larger holds out to the left. Bowden Doors is a crag made for soloing and bouldering and Russett Groove is not to be left off anyone's itinerary. The line is obvious. There are other routes that can be included in your circuit and many are of great worth, but it is seldom that such good climbing is found at this grade. Do it!

Information

The following pages list each route, and I have also included any relevant information so that you can find out the grade, any restrictions, and so on, and can look it up in the guidebook. Along with the name of the guidebook is a code for the relevant publisher according to the following key:

CC   Climbers Club
BMC   BMC
CO   Constable
FRCC   Fell and Rock Climbing Club
D   Diadem
C   Cordee
YMC   Yorkshire Mountaineering Club
NMC   Northumberland Mountaineering Club
FAX   Vertical Brain Rock Fax

I have only included British grades as this book is about climbing in England and Wales. A relevant comparison with French and American grades, if possible, is as follows:

U.K.	French	American 5
D	–	2/3
VD	1	4/5
S	2	6
HS	3	7
VS	4	8
HVS	5	9
E1	6a	10a/10b
E2	6b	10c/10d
E3	6b+/6c	11a/11b
E4	6c+/7a	11c/11d
E5	7a+/7b	12a/12b
E6	7b+/7c/7c+	12c/12d/13a
E7	8a/8a+	13b/13c
E8	8b/8b+	13d/14a
E9	8c	14b

KEY TO AREAS

SEE   South-east England
SWA   Swanage
CHE   Cheddar
DEV   Devon
LUN   Lundy
COR   Cornwall
PEM   Pembroke
NW   North Wales
P   Peak District
Y   Yorkshire
LAK   Lake District
NTH   Northumberland

Note: FFA = first free ascent

Route		Grade	Area	Crag	Length	First Ascent	Guidebook
1	Infidel	6a	SEE	High Rocks	40ft	M. Fowler 1970s	Southern Sandstone CC
2	Kraite Arete	6b	SEE	High Rocks	30ft	M. Boysen 1980s	Southern Sandstone CC
3	Second Generation	6c	SEE	High Rocks	50ft	J. Sharpe 1990	Southern Sandstone CC
4	Avernus	S	SWA	Subliminal	70ft	M. Hurn F. Higgins D.W. Partridge 1971	Swanage CC South West Climbs D
5	Finale Groove	HVS 4c	SWA	Boulder Ruckle	150ft	G. Smith D. Hadlum 1966	Swanage CC South West Climbs D
6	Ocean Boulevard	E3 5b	SWA	Boulder Ruckle	130ft	K. Turner N. Buckley S. Bartlett 1979	Swanage CC South West Climbs D
7	Lean Machine	E5 6a	SWA	Boulder Ruckle	130ft	M. Crocker J. Robertson 1983	Swanage CC South West Climbs D
8	Polaris	E4 6a	SWA	Blackers Hole	215ft	A. Strapcans G. Jenkin F. Farrell 1979	Swanage CC
9	Conger	E1 5c	SWA	Fisherman's West	100ft	R. Crewe FFA F. Farrell 1979	Swanage CC South West Climbs D
10	Coronation Street	E1 5c	CHE	High Rocks	390ft	C. Bonnington J. Cleare A. Greenbank 1965	Avon and Cheddar CC South West Climbs D
11	Bird of Paradise	E6 6b	CHE	Sunset Buttress	290ft	R. S. Dearman D. Lester (aid) 1969 FFA M. Crocker D. Ardon 1986	Avon and Cheddar CC South West Climbs D
12	Empire of the Sun	E5 6a	DEV	Anstey's Cove	90ft	N. White/P. Bull A. Turner 1988	South West Climbs D
13	Cider Soak	E7 6c	DEV	Anstey's Cove	50ft	N. White	No current guide
14	Suspension Flake	VS 4c	DEV	Hounds Tor	45ft		No current guide
15	Sacré Coeur	E2 5c	DEV	Blackchurch	110ft	P. Littlejohn H. Clarke 1974	North Devon and Cornwall CC South West Climbs D
16	Fay	E5 6a	DEV	Lower Sharpnose	120ft	P. Littlejohn M. Hardwick 1986	North Devon and Cornwall CC South West Climbs D
17	Eroica	E2 6a	COR	Pentire	210ft	P. Littlejohn G. Morton 1971 FFA P. Livesey J. Lawrence	North Devon and Cornwall CC South West Climbs D
18	Darkinbad the Brightdayler	E5 6a	COR	Pentire	205ft	P. Littlejohn I. Duckworth 1972 FFA R. Fawcett P. Gomersall 1976	North Devon and Cornwall CC South West Climbs D

Route		Grade	Area	Crag	Length	First Ascent	Guidebook
19	Doorpost	HS	COR	Bosigran	210ft	B. Biven H. Peck P. Biven 1955	Bosigran CC South West Climbs D
20	Black Slab	D	COR	Bosigran	105ft	C.F. Kirkus P.S. Fallows 1938	Bosigran CC South West Climbs D
21	Dream Liberator	E3 5c	COR	Bosigran	200ft	M. Guilliard R. O'B. Wilson FFA R. Fawcett P. Livesey 1976	Bosigran CC South West Climbs D
22	Saxon	HVS 5a	COR	Carn Kenidjack	150ft	P. Littlejohn S. Jones 1974	Bosigran CC South West Climbs D
23	Last Dancer	E4 6a	COR	Cormorant Promontory Land's End	125ft	R. Edwards M. Edwards 1985	Bosigran CC South West Climbs D
24	Stone Boom	E1 5c	COR	Pordenack	100ft	R. Edwards R. Perriment 1980	Chair Ladder CC
25	Inter Space	E4 6a	COR	Paradise Wall	100ft	R. Edwards M. Edwards 1982	Chair Ladder CC South West Climbs D
26	Pegasus	HS	COR	Chair Ladder	185ft	J. Deacon and party 1955	Chair Ladder CC South West Climbs D
27	Terrier's Tooth	VD	COR	Chair	150ft		Chair Ladder CC South West Climbs D
28	The Cull	E3 5c	COR	Bass Point	100ft	S. Bell S. Bishop P. O'Sullivan 1986	North Devon and Cornwall CC South West Climbs D
29	Arucaria	E6 6c	LUN	St Johns Stone	150ft	N. White N. Foster 1991	No current guidebook
30	Satan's Slip	E1 5a	LUN	Devil's Slide	320ft	L.P. Fatti D. Ward 1970	South West Climbs D
31	Star Gate	E3 5c	PEM	Mother Carey's	130ft	P. Littlejohn R. Harrison 1977	Pembroke CC
32	Rock Idol	HVS 5b	PEM	Mother Carey's	140ft	P. Littlejohn R. Harrison 1977	Pembroke CC
33	The Butcher	E3 5c	PEM	St Govans	80ft	P. Littlejohn M. Winteringham B. Winteringham 1980	Pembroke CC
34	Trevallen Pillar	E4 6a	PEM	Trevallen	150ft	J. De Montjoye I. Parsons 1981	Pembroke CC
35	Pleasure Dome	E3 5c	PEM	Stennis Head	150ft	P. Littlejohn J. Perrin 1980	Pembroke CC
36	Bloody Sunday	E4 6a	PEM	Huntsman's Leap	140ft	A. Sharp P. Lewis 1979	Pembroke CC
37	Souls	E6 6c	PEM	Huntsman's Leap	130ft	G. Gibson 1985	Pembroke CC
38	Lucky Strike	E2 5b	PEM	Rusty Walls	130ft	P. Littlejohn C. Heard 1980	Pembroke CC

Route		Grade	Area	Crag	Length	First Ascent	Guidebook
39	Pigs on the Wing	HVS 5b	PEM	Triple Overhang Buttress	190ft	C. Heard S. Lewis 1979	Pembroke CC
40	Axle Attack	E5 6a	NW	Pen Trwyn	80ft	M. Griffiths L. McGinley 1981	North Wales Limestone CC North Wales Limestone FAX
41	Statement of Youth	E7 6b	NW	Lower Pen Trwyn	75ft	B. Moon 1984	North Wales Limestone CC North Wales Limestone FAX
42	Liquid Amber	E9 7a	NW	Lower Pen Trwyn	75ft	J. Moffat 1990	North Wales Limestone FAX
43	Grooved Arete	VD	NW	Tryfan	865ft	E.W. Steeple and Party 1911	Ogwen and Carneddau CC Snowdonia CO
44	Tennis Shoe	S	NW	Idwal Slabs	465ft	N. Odell 1919	Ogwen and Carneddau CC Snowdonia CO
45	Direct Route	VS 5a	NW	Dinas Mot	245ft	C. Kirkus J. Dodd 1930	Llanberis CC Snowdonia CO
46	Left Wall	E2 5c	NW	Dinas Cromlech	140ft	R. Moseley J. Smith J. Sutherland 1956 FFA A. Garlick 1970	Llanberis CC Snowdonia CO
47	Cemetery Gates	E1 5c	NW	Dinas Cromlech	170ft	J. Brown D. Whillans 1951	Llanberis CC Snowdonia CO
48	Main Wall	HS	NW	Cryn Las	465ft	J. Cooke P. Roberts 1935	Llanberis CC Snowdonia CO
49	The Rainbow of Recalcitrance	E6 6b	NW	Rainbow Slab	200ft	J. Silvester M. Lyndon 1984	Slate CC Snowdonia CO
50	Central Sadness	E5 6a	NW	California Hole	220ft	J. Silvester C. Dale 1986	Slate CC Snowdonia CO
51	The Dark Half	E7 6c	NW	Manatese Level	60ft	N. Harms 1989	Slate CC
52	Comes the Dervish	E3 5c	NW	Vivian Quarry	130ft	S. Haston 1982	Slate CC Snowdonia CO
53	The Axe	E4 6a	NW	Clogwyn D'ur Arddu	150ft	P. Littlejohn C. King 1979	Clogwyn D'ur Arddu CC Snowdonia CC
54	Outside Edge	VD	NW	Cwm Silyn	390ft	J. Edwards C. Palmer	Tremadoc CC Snowdonia CO
55	Craig Dhu Wall	HS	NW	Craig Y Castell	200ft	J. Cunningham W. Smith P. Vaughan	Tremadoc CC Snowdonia CO
56	Vector	E2 5c	NW	Craig Bwlch y Moch	250ft	J. Brown C.E. Davies	Tremadoc CC Snowdonia CO
57	Symphony Crack	D	NW	Rhoscolyn	60ft	D. Durkan J. Baker 1970	Gogarth CC Snowdonia CO
58	The Moon	E3 5c	NW	Yellow Walls	260ft	E. Drummond A. Barely 1971 FFA A. Sharp 1974	Gogarth CC Snowdonia CO
59	Hunger	E5 6a	NW	Main Cliff	300ft	P. Littlejohn C. King 1978	Gogarth CC

Route		Grade	Area	Crag	Length	First Ascent	Guidebook
60	Dream of White Horses	HVS 4c	NW	Wen Zawn	500ft	E. Drummond D. Pearce 1968	Gogarth CC Snowdonia CO
61	Britomartis	HVS 4c	NW	Wen Zawn	190ft	D. Alcock G. Rogan 1967	Gogarth CC Snowdonia CO
62	The Hollow Man	E7 6b	NW	North Stack	120ft	A. Pollitt J. Dawes 1986	Gogarth CC
63	Valkyrie	VS	P	Roaches	120ft	P. Harding A. Bowden Black 1946	Staffordshire Gritstone BMC Peak District CO
64	Pedestal Crack	VD	P	Roaches	90ft	M. Wood 1922	Staffordshire Gritstone BMC Peak District CO
65	Sloth	HVS 4c	P	Roaches	90ft	D. Whillans J. Brown 1954	Staffordshire Gritstone BMC Peak District CO
66	Darius	E2 5c	P	High Tor	160ft	P. Livesey 1974	Peak Limestone South BMC Peak District CO Peak Limestone FAX
67	Body Machine	E6 6c	P	Raven Tor	80ft	R. Fawcett 1984	Peak Limestone Chee Dale BMC Peak Limestone FAX
68	Mecca	E8 6c	P	Raven Tor	40ft	M. Atkinson 1988	Peak Limestone FAX
69	Moonwalk	E4 6a	P	Curbar	50ft	J. Allen N. Stokes M. Stokes 1976	Froggat BMC Peak District CO
70	Chequers Buttress	HVS 5a	P	Froggatt	40ft	J. Gosling M. Simpkins 1962	Froggat BMC Peak District CO
71	Beau Geste	E7 6c	P	Froggatt	40ft	J. Woodward 1983	Froggat BMC Peak District CO
72	Pebble Mill	E5 6b	P	Burbage South	45ft	J. Allen 1976	Froggat BMC Peak District CO
73	Mutiny Crack	VS 4c	P	Burbage North	40ft	E. Byrom D. Milner 1934	Froggat BMC
74	Archangel	E3 5c	P	Stanage	65ft	E. Drummond H. Green Armitage 1972	Stanage BMC Peak District CO
75	Edge Lane	E5 5c	P	Millstone	120ft	A. McHardy 1974	Froggat BMC Peak District CO
76	London Wall	E5 6a	P	Millstone	70ft	J. Allen S. Bancroft 1975	Froggat BMC Peak District CO
77	The Rasp	E2 5b	P	Higgar Tor	55ft	J. Brown D. Whillans 1956	Froggat BMC Peak District CO
78	Sirplum	HVS 4c	P	Plum Buttress	180ft	R. Dearman R. Brown 1964	Peak Limestone Chee Dale BMC Peak District CO Peak Limestone FAX
79	High Noon	E4 6a	Y	Caley	50ft	A. Manson M. Hammill 1975	Yorkshire Gritstone YMC Northern England CO
80	Great Western	HVS 5a	Y	Almscliff	60ft	A. Dolphin R. Heap 1943	Yorkshire Gritstone YMC Northern England CO

Route		Grade	Area	Crag	Length	First Ascent	Guidebook
81	Wellington Crack	E4 5c	Y	Ilkley	50ft	P. Livesey J. Sheard 1973 FFA R. Fawcett 1978	Yorkshire Gritstone YMC Northern England CO
82	The Ashes	E6 6b	Y	Kilnsey	75ft	G. Weigand 1989	Yorkshire Limestone YMC Yorkshire Limestone FAX
83	Supercool	E7 6c	Y	Gordale	80ft	M. Atkinson 1988	Yorkshire Limestone YMC Yorkshire Limestone FAX
84	Obsession	E6 6b	Y	Malham	60ft	S. Lewis 1984	Yorkshire Limestone YMC Yorkshire Limestone FAX Northern England CO
85	The Groove	E7 6b	Y	Malham	120ft	J. Dunne 1988	Yorkshire Limestone YMC Yorkshire Limestone FAX Northern England CO
86	Zoolook	E7 6c	Y	Malham	80ft	R. Fawcett 1985	Yorkshire Limestone YMC Yorkshire Limestone FAX Northern England CO
87	Overhanging Bastion	VS 4c	LAK	Castle Rock	270ft	R. Birkett C. Williamson L. Muscroft 1939	Buttermere and Eastern Crags FRCC Lake District CO
88	Hell's Wall	E6 6c	LAK	Bowderstone Crag	100ft	R. Fawcett 1983	Borrowdale FRCC Lake District CO
89	Troutdale Pinnacle	S	LAK	Black Crag	360ft	F. Mallinson R. Mayson 1914	Borrowdale FRCC Lake District CO
90	White Noise	E3 5c	LAK	Reecastle	100ft	J. Lamb R. McHaffe 1978	Borrowdale FRCC Lake District CO
91	Praying Mantis	E1 5c	LAK	Goat Crag	260ft	L. Brown J. Bradshaw 1965	Borrowdale FRCC Lake District CO
92	Tophet Wall	HS	LAK	Napes Crag	265ft	H. Kelly R. Pritchard 1923	Gable FRCC Lake District CO
93	Botterill's Slab	VS 4c	LAK	Scafell	235ft	F. Botterill H. Williamson J. Grant 1903	Scafell Dow and Eskdale FRCC Lake District CO
94	Borderline	E6 6c	LAK	Scafell East	250ft	C. Sowden M. Berzins 1986	Scafell, Dow and Eskdale FRCC
95	Roaring Silence	E3 5c	LAK	Scafell East	250ft	B. Berzins J. Lamb M. Berzins 1979	Scafell, Dow and Eskdale FRCC
96	Eliminate A	VS 4c	LAK	Dow Crag	375ft	H. Gross G. Basterfield 1923	Scarfell, Dow and Eskdale FRCC Lake District CO
97	C Ordinary Route	D	LAK	Dow Crag	360ft	C. and A. Woodhouse 1904	Scafell, Dow and Eskdale FRCC Lake District CO
98	Tigers Wall	VS 4b	NTH	Bowden Doors	35ft		Northumberland NMC Northern England CO
99	Poseidon Adventure	E4 6a	NTH	Bowden Doors	40ft	S. Blake	Northumberland NMC Northern England CO
100	Russett Groove	D	NTH	Bowden Doors	30ft		Northumberland NMC Northern England CO

ANALYSIS

To save the interested reader searching through this list I have done a little analysis.

Routes in Various Areas

South-east England	3
Swanage	6
Cheddar	2
Devon	5
Lundy	2
Cornwall	13
Total south and west	**31**
Pembroke	9
North Wales	23
Total Wales	**32**
Peak District	16
Yorkshire	8
Lake District	10
Northumberland	3
Total north	**37**

TOTAL   100

The shortest and easiest route is Russett Groove: 30ft, grade Diff.
The longest route is Grooved Arete: 865ft.
The oldest route is Botterill's Slab: climbed in 1903.
The hardest route is Liquid Amber: E9 7a.
The most recent route is Arucaria: first climbed in 1991.
The most necky route is Hollow Man: E7 6b.
The person who has made the most first ascents in this book is Pat Littlejohn: twelve out of the 100.

The routes are spread in these proportions between the grades:

D	4	E5	10
VD	4	E6	9
S	3	E7	8
HS	5	E8	1
VS	8	E9	1
HVS	10		
E1	6	6a	1
E2	7	6b	1
E3	11	6c	1
E4	10		

GRADED LIST

Here, in descending order of difficulty, is a graded list of the 100 best routes in England and Wales.

E9	Liquid Amber	E9	7a
E8	Mecca (The Mid-life Crisis)	E8	6c
E7	Supercool	E7	6c
	The Dark Half	E7	6c
	Cider Soak	E7	6c
	The Hollow Man	E7	6b
	Beau Geste	E7	6c
	Zoolook	E7	6c
	The Groove	E7	6b
	Statement of Youth	E7	6b
E6	Souls	E6	6c
	Arucaria	E6	6c
	Second Generation		6c
	Borderline	E6	6c
	Hell's Wall	E6	6c
	Bird of Paradise	E6	6b
	The Ashes	E6	6b
	Body Machine	E6	6b
	Obsession	E6	6b
	The Rainbow of Recalcitrance	E6	6b
E5	Edge Lane	E5	5c
	Lean Machine	E5	6a
	London Wall	E5	6a
	Hunger	E5	6a
	Central Sadness	E5	6a
	Empire of the Sun	E5	6a
	Axle Attack	E5	6a
	Kraite Arete		6b
	Pebble Mill	E5	6b
	Darkinbad the Brightdayler	E5	6a
	Fay	E5	6a
E4	High Noon	E4	6b
	Poseidon Adventure	E4	6a
	Wellington Crack	E4	5c
	Infidel		6a
	Moonwalk	E4	6b
	Polaris	E4	6a
	Inter Space	E4	6a
	Last Dancer	E4	6a
	The Axe	E4	6a
	Trevallen Pillar	E4	6a
	Bloody Sunday	E4	6a

E3	Archangel	E3	5c
	Pleasure Dome	E3	5c
	Dream Liberator	E3	5c
	Comes the Dervish	E3	5c
	The Cull	E3	5c
	Star Gate	E3	5c
	The Moon	E3	5c
	Roaring Silence	E3	5c
	Ocean Boulevard	E3	5b
	White Noise	E3	5c
	The Butcher	E3	5c
E2	The Rasp	E2	5b
	Eroica	E2	6a
	Left Wall	E2	5c
	Darius	E2	5c
	Vector	E2	5c
	Sacré Coeur	E2	5c
	Lucky Strike	E2	5b
E1	Conger	E1	5c
	Coronation Street	E1	5c
	Stone Boom	E1	5c
	Cemetery Gates	E1	5c
	Praying Mantis	E1	5c
	Satan's Slip	E1	5a
HVS	Sloth	HVS	4c
	Rock Idol	HVS	5b
	Great Western	HVS	4c
	Pigs on the Wing	HVS	5b
	Dream of White Horses	HVS	4c
	Sirplum	HVS	4c
	Saxon	HVS	5a
	Finale Groove	HVS	4c
	Britomartis	HVS	4c
	Chequers Buttress	HVS	5a

VS	Valkyrie	VS	5a
	Eliminate A	VS	4c
	Overhanging Bastion	VS	4c
	Suspension Flake	VS	4c
	Direct Route	VS	5a
	Botterill's Slab	VS	4c
	Mutiny Crack	VS	4c
	Tigers Wall	VS	4b
HS	Main Wall	HS	4b
	Craig Dhu Wall	HS	4b
	Pegasus	HS	4a
	Doorpost	HS	4a
	Tophet Wall	HS	4a
S	Avernus	S	3c
	Troutdale Pinnacle	S	4a
	Tennis Shoe	S	4a
VD	Grooved Arete	VD	
	Terrier's Tooth	VD	
	Pedestal Crack	VD	
	Outside Edge	VD	
D	Symphony Crack	D	
	Black Slab	D	
	C Ordinary Route	D	
	Russett Groove	D	

Glossary

For the uninitiated, climbing terminology, like that of any other specialist subject, is a mystery. In the bulk of this book I have tried to avoid using jargon but some is inevitable. It is the beauty of the English language that new words can be created to fit new situations and new meanings attributed to existing words or phrases. In this section I shall try to explain rock climbing terminology. Most is fairly straightforward, some not so and some deliberately humorous. I have used two sources of reference: Paul Williams' Llanberis guidebook and Ian Horrocks' article, 'Speak No Evil' in *On The Edge,* no. 8.

Abseil   To descend in a controlled manner using a rope, and, more usually these days, some form of friction device.

Aid climbing   To climb a piece of rock using means other than the natural holds.

Arete   An edge of rock with a drop on both sides.

Babbling brooks   A rock climbing photographer.

Badger's head   A smooth, rounded hold mostly found on sandstone crags. Hence the expression 'Slap the badger's head!'

Bale out   To get going before the going gets tough. Or to leave the crag and go home/to the pub/café/amusement arcade and so on.

Belay   To hold the ropes and stop someone hitting the ground, or a place part-way up a cliff where the climber attaches himself while his partner climbs.

Belayer   The person who does the belaying.

Bolt   Bolts come in several forms. Basically, a bolt is an item screwed or glued into a hole in the crag that has previously been drilled by the climber; a hanger for clipping the rope is then attached.

Bolt ladder   A line of bolts up a crag.

Bomb proof   Reference to protection that has no chance of coming out in the event of a fall.

Bonnington   To grow a beard and publicize yourself until no British climbing event is complete without your seal of approval.

Bosch   A cordless hammer drill used for drilling bolt holes.

Bumbly   The sort of person who does not like bolts. A derogatory term used in connection with people who are not very good at climbing.

Camelot   Expensive American version of a friend.

Camping   An activity only carried out by bumblies and punters. Real climbers doss.

Cellar   A place you go to train.

Chalk   What you climb on along most of the south coast, or what you put in your chalk bag to keep your hands from getting too sweaty.

Chalk bag   A little bag for putting chalk in.

Chop route   A route on which failure will result in certain death.

Cleaning   Either preparing a route prior to an ascent (clearing away dirt, vegetation, loose rock and so on) or getting the gear out of a route once it has been climbed.

Cliff   A vertical piece of real estate.

Clip   To clip the rope into a karabiner.

Crater   The hole in the ground you'll make if you hit it.

Crag   The climbing venue. Crags are generally smaller than cliffs.

Crag rat   Something student climbers call themselves.

Crank   To pull very hard on a hold. Hence the expression 'crank till your arms fall off!'

Crimp   To hold a small hold tightly.

Crimp nasty   A person who is very good at crimping, for example, Paul Pritchard.

Cruise   To climb in a smooth controlled manner and make it look very easy.
Crux   The hardest part of a climb.

Dog   To climb a route with rests on the protection. Hence the expression 'on the Dog'.
Doss   Sleeping somewhere where you do not have to pay and can be quite untidy and smelly, such as a friend's house, a football stadium, park bench, cave and so on.
Dyno   A controlled dynamic move for a hold. Very useful as it saves energy.

Edge   A small positive hold.
Ethics   Something very personal that organizations are always trying to define, which is impossible as they change with the tide of progress.

Fall   Something everyone does, some more than others. At first frightening, then less so unless you get it wrong.
Figure of four   A horribly technical move that involves looping your leg over your hand while it is holding on, used to gain more height. Most people prefer to dyno, which is easier but less accurate.
Figure of eight   A friction device that is used for abseiling or belaying, which, peculiarly, is figure-of-eight shaped.
Flash   To climb a route in one go from the bottom to the top on the first attempt.
Flexible friends   Not Access cards, but camming protection devices with flexible stalks.
Friends   Something you had before you started climbing, or a camming protection device.
Frigging   To climb a route in bad style, pulling on the gear, maybe, or resting, or falling off a lot.
Flying time   The time spent while falling.
Fumble clip   To fumble with the karabiner or rope when clipping. Can have nasty consequences.

Gear   Another word for protection.
Gripped   Something that happens to us all, usually when there is the prospect of injury or other nasty things happening.
Gripper clipper   A piece of protection that is difficult to clip, but where the failure to do so results in some form of injury.

Gym   A place to build up those lovely muscles.

Hammock   Something to lie in while belaying.
Hang Dog(ging)   The climber's expression after failing to redpoint a sports route, or, hanging around on the bolts working out the moves.
Harness   A multi-coloured webbing contraption that goes around the legs and waist. You tie the rope into this and it is much more comfortable than just tying the rope around your waist. Will be laughed at on southern sandstone crags.
Helmet   A hard hat that gets in your way when climbing, but might save your life if someone knocks a rock down from above.
Hex   An old-fashioned type of camming protection device.
Hilti   Another type of cordless hammer drill. More expensive than, and superior to, a Bosch.
Hauling   Something they do in America and Norway.

In Situ   Protection that is permanently in place.

Jumars   Mechanical clamps that enable you to climb a rope.

Karabiners   Metal rings with a spring-loaded bar which you can clip into things.

Layback   A method of climbing something sideways.
Lower off   To descend to the ground on the rope with your belayer taking the strain.
Lunge   Dyno in an uncontrolled manner.

Necky   A dangerous climb.
Nut   Anyone who climbs on the Red Walls at Gogarth, or an old-fashioned type of rock.
Ninja   A type of climbing slipper.

On Sight   To climb a route with no prior knowledge. An on-sight flash is the best form of ascent.
Overhanging   Any rock at an angle over ninety degrees.

Path   An easy climb, or a hard climb that the ascensionist wants everyone to think he found easy.
Peg   A more socially acceptable piece of *in situ* protection.
Piton   French word for peg.

Power The strength to do hard moves. Hence the expressions 'I was powered out' and 'Keep the power on and sort the feet out!'

Protection Interesting little metal devices that fit into cracks and pockets. The rope is attached to them with a karabiner and they stop you hitting the ground. Or something like that.

Pump A type of plimsoll/trainer, or what happens to your muscles when the going gets steep, the holds get too small or you get frightened. Pumping out is a popular way of getting fit.

Punter Climber who is not known to the Llanberis/Sheffield mafia.

Quick draw A piece of webbing with karabiners at each end that goes from the protection to the rope.

Radical Something to say when someone does something a bit different.

Rap As abseil.

Redpoint To climb a route from the bottom to the top without falling off or resting, having tried it before or practised the moves.

Rock What we climb on, or a protection device. Basically a metal wedge on a loop of wire.

Rockover Getting your weight over one foot on a high hold, then standing up on it with a lack of hand holds.

Roof A bit of rock sticking out horizontally.

RP A very small rock-type thing.

Runner What you do when you leave a campsite, or another word for protection.

Sequence A series of technical moves.

Skateboard What takes over from climbing if you cannot afford a racing car/bike.

Slab Easy angled rock. What is easy angled depends on the climber.

Slap Where you literally slap a hold hoping your hand will stay there.

Sling A piece of webbing in a loop which can be used to extend runners or loop over spikes.

Slipper A very light slip-on climbing shoe.

Smear To friction with your boot when there isn't a foothold.

Smee Not very good.

Solo To climb without ropes.

Stance The place where you takes a belay.

Stitch plate A friction device used for abseiling or belaying.

Stick To hold a rounded hold when a bit pumped. Hence the expression 'Stick It!'

Take What you shout at your belayer when you are next to some protection and want to rest on it rather than fall off above.

Tiny A small hold.

Trade route A popular climb.

Tri cam A silly kind of protection.

Topo A diagrammatic guide to a crag.

Udge To move up a very little way.

Wall A vertical piece of rock, or a place to train.

Wallnut A more developed type of rock.

Wired Knowing all the moves on a climb so well you can cruise it every time.

Yo-Yo To lower to the ground after a fall and then climb the route without pulling the ropes back down.

Zippy A man with a mission. Usually found at Raven Tor.

Index of Climbs

Archangel, 111
Arucaria, 49
Ashes, The, 121
Avernus, 19
Axe, The, 84
Axle Attack, 65

Beau Geste, 108
Bird of Paradise, 26
Black Slab, 36
Bloody Sunday, 61
Body Machine, 103
Borderline, 140
Botterill's Slab, 138
Britomartis, 96
Butcher, The, 57

Cemetery Gates, 78
Central Sadness, 81
Chequers Buttress, 107
Cider Soak, 28
Comes the Dervish, 83
Conger, 24
C Ordinary Route, 144
Coronation Street, 25
Craig Dhu Wall, 86
Cull, The, 48

Darius, 102
Dark Half, The, 82
Darkinbad the Brightdayler, 34
Direct Route, 74
Doorpost, 35
Dream Liberator, 38
Dream of White Horses, 95

Edge Lane, 112
Eliminate A, 142
Empire of the Sun, 27
Eroica, 33

Fay, 32
Finale Groove, 20

Great Western, 119
Groove, The, 125
Grooved Arete, 70

Hell's Wall, 129
High Noon, 118
Hollow Man, The, 97
Hunger, 92

Infidel, 16
Inter Space, 44

Kraite Arete, 17

Last Dancer, 41
Lean Machine, 22
Left Wall, 76
Liquid Amber, 69
London Wall, 113
Lucky Strike, 63

Main Wall, 79
Mecca (The Mid-Life Crisis), 104
Moon, The, 91
Moonwalk, 106
Mutiny Crack, 110

Obsession, 123
Ocean Boulevard, 21
Outside Edge, 85
Overhanging Bastion, 128

Pebble Mill, 109
Pedestal Crack, 100
Pegasus, 45
Pigs on the Wing, 64
Pleasure Dome, 60

Polaris, 23
Poseidon Adventure, 146
Praying Mantis, 134

Rainbow of Recalcitrance, The, 80
Rasp, The, 114
Roaring Silence, 141
Rock Idol, 56
Russett Groove, 148

Sacré Coeur, 30
Satan's Slip, 50
Saxon, 40
Second Generation, 18
Sirplum, 116
Sloth, 101
Souls, 62
Star Gate, 54
Statement of Youth, 66
Stone Boom, 42
Supercool, 122
Suspension Flake, 29
Symphony Crack, 90

Tennis Shoe, 72
Terrier's Tooth, 46
Tigers Wall, 145
Tophet Wall, 136
Trevallen Pillar, 58
Troutdale Pinnacle, 130

Valkyrie, 99
Vector, 88

Wellington Crack, 120
White Noise, 132

Zoolook, 126